FANTOGRAPHY

SAN DIEGO BASEBALL

MY DIAMOND GIRL. I was married on October 9, 1976, after the baseball season had concluded. I promised myself that if I were to ever get married it would be at home plate on some playground. Fortunately for me, I met the girl of my dreams during my second year with the Padres. Patti Hampson and I were married at home plate at San Diego Stadium. It was the first baseball wedding at the ballpark. (Author's collection.)

PLAY GROUND. After Sunday games, I and a few other employees would go down on the field that had just been the site of a major-league game. This snapshot of me pitching is one of my favorite photographs. The ground crew took down the pitcher's mound due to a Monday night Chargers game the next day. We played until it got dark, just like when we were kids. (Author's collection.)

FRONT COVER: Clockwise from the top, the 1992 MLB All-Star Game was played on July 14, 1992, at Jack Murphy Stadium (Tom Larwin); "Suitcase" Simpson played for the 1950 PCL Padres and clouted 33 homers that season before playing in the big leagues (Kay E. Scozzafava); the San Diego Chicken is in a class by himself when it comes to entertaining fans around the world, but he started his career in San Diego (Freddie Obligado); while earning eight batting titles, Tony Gwynn (hand in hand with his daughter and son on a Padres family-day softball game) is "Mr. Padre" and became a Hall of Famer in 2007 (Larry Carpa); Trevor Hoffman is the greatest reliever in National League history with 601 saves (Larry Carpa).

BACK COVER: From left to right, for the first four years of his Hall of Fame career, Ozzie Smith delighted fans on the field and was a favorite of Laurie Larwin and Tom Larwin Jr. (Tom Larwin); as the "voice of the Padres," Jerry Coleman spent over 40 years describing Padres ball games to the delight of fans and was inducted into the broadcasters wing of the National Baseball Hall of Fame in 2005 (Madres); longtime Fallbrook resident Duke Snider had a bowling alley in the early 1960s that was considered by many to be very cool (Jack and Susie Nopal).

BACKGROUND: This 1960s photograph of the Westgate Ball Park scoreboard had two oversize Breast O' Chicken Tuna Fish cans that dominated what appears to be a very small clock and line score. (Luis Marlin.)

FANTOGRAPHY

SAN DIEGO BASEBALL

Andy Strasberg

ARCADIA
PUBLISHING

Published by Arcadia Publishing
Charleston, South Carolina

Printed in the United States of America

Library of Congress Control Number: 2013952363

For all general information, please contact Arcadia Publishing:
Telephone 843-853-2070
Fax 843-853-0044
E-mail sales@arcadiapublishing.com
For customer service and orders:
Toll-Free 1-888-313-2665

Visit us on the Internet at www.arcadiapublishing.com

For more about Fantography or to submit a photograph, please visit www.fantography.com

CONTENTS

ACKNOWLEDGMENTS

I had the privilege of working for the San Diego Padres, starting in 1975, and had many conversations with then–Padres owner Ray Kroc. Ray made a point that at no time should anyone in the organization thank fans for their support. He didn't like the word *support*. He often said he didn't need anyone's support and clarified that he was immensely appreciative of the fans' *participation*—the word he wanted all of us to use. It made sense to me, and I would like to continue that legacy of thanking the following individuals for their participation in making this book become a reality.

For their confidence and love: Patti Strasberg and Hazel (our canine daughter).

For their steadfast faith in me and the Fantography project: Ted Giannoulas, Steve Smith, John Boggs, Randy Maris, and Andrew Maris.

For their unwavering and consistent friendship: Jerry and Maggie Coleman, Arnie and Debra Cardillo, Bob and Anna Lee Serrano, Peter and Joyce Briante, Jim Gold, Dick Freeman, Amanda and Gary Hamels, Belinda Bird, Bill and Alice Habeger, Jeff Prescott, Kathy Johnson, Doug and Joy Harvey, Jim and Janice Healy, Susan Mendolia, Lloyd Kuritsky, Rob Johnson, Charlie Oates, Joe Milchen, Aracely Segura, Sean Kinyon, Li-An and Jeff Meredith, Ron and Christy Seaver, John Freeman, Drew Schlosberg, Jeff Silberman, Jeff Idelson, Tim Wiles, Jim Gates, and Tom Shieber.

For their hands on participation: Doug Gilmore, Duane Dimock, Daniel M. Novis, David Kent, Howard Frank, Joe Milchen, Pete Meisner, Monnee Tong, Robert Warmack, Mike Metzger, Bill Swank, Mark Macrae, Joe Podesta, Geoff Belinfante, and Rich Domich.

The dedicated and talented Arcadia Publishing All-Star team: Jeff Ruetsche, Alyssa Jones, Mike Litchfield, and Rob Kangas.

For the talented wordsmiths who contributed: to begin with, Ernie Kovacs, who never hesitated to get involved. I wish there was a better word than "thanks" for the incredible assistance Jack McCabe provided. It is Jack who lent his writing skills when I often needed wording enhanced, sentences reconstructed, and paragraphs moved and edited so there was continuity in my written thoughts.

Early Fantography contributors who provided me with their extensive photo collections: Tom Larwin, Larry Carpa, Gary Holdinghausen, Pati and Rick Zambori, Fred O. Rodgers, and the incredible San Diego Madres organization. The Madres is made up of women and men who love baseball and their community and whose mission is to provide all children of San Diego County the opportunity to play baseball and softball.

For any of the success I experienced at the Padres it was because of the guidance, talent, dedication, cooperation, trust, and hard work of those Padres employees who worked with me.

Last in this long litany of persons deserving my gratitude—but certainly not the least—are all of the fans who sent me incredible personal and poignant baseball snapshots. From the outset, my goal was to share the San Diego baseball experience from the perspective of you, the fan, as seen through your camera lens finder. I wanted to shine the spotlight on all of you. There was something important enough about your baseball experience that caused you to bring a camera to a game, take photographs, and then develop and preserve them as part of your family history. Thank you for sharing those memories and experiences with me, and now with the reader of this labor of love.

INTRODUCTION

The single most significant and fortunate thing in my professional life is that I was able to make a living working in the sport I loved most as a boy growing up: baseball. This was done even though my mother was concerned about my future and would often announce to anyone who would listen, "If Andrew only knew his schoolwork as well as he knows baseball, because baseball is not going to provide him a living later on in his life."

For 22 years, from 1975 to 1996, I worked for the San Diego Padres, and since then I have been able to make a living consulting with teams, players, and businesses related to baseball, as well as represent a broadcaster, a Hall of Fame umpire, and a talented guy who literally runs around in a chicken costume. I have also written a couple of books about baseball, as well as a one-man, one-act play that has baseball as a theme.

In 1997, I started thinking about the unpublished, hidden story of baseball through the snapshots fans have taken of their baseball experience. I pursued it as a project and called it Fantography. The premise for Fantography is quite simple: gathering amateur snapshots fans have taken of their baseball experiences in both the major and minor leagues relating to San Diego. The only qualifiers are that the fan must not be a professional photographer and the photograph is not of game action. Take a close look, and you will see almost no photograph in this book is of a baseball game when a player his hitting, catching, running, or throwing a baseball. Despite never having a pitcher hurl a no-hit game, never having a player hit for the cycle, and still waiting for a World Series championship, the Padres have produced three different Cy Young Award winners, an eight-time batting champion, and a number of Hall of Famers who at one time wore a Padres uniform. San Diego baseball fans are loyal and enthusiastic, and their photographs reflect their love of the game. This is really about the fans, for the fans, and from the fans.

Fan*tog*ra*phy

Definition: the art of capturing images of a subject by amateur photographers who are enthusiasts of the subject matter.

Mission: to obtain and archive photographs of professional baseball taken by fans of the game—photographs most likely not seen before by the public. The unique relationship the institution of sport has created between itself and its fans is perhaps best represented by and through professional baseball. The enduring popularity of the sport is supported by the fact it has been woven into the very fabric of American popular culture over the last 150 years. Baseball remains the quintessential summer game, amplified once school is out of session and families take vacations. Unlike many other sports, the pace of a professional baseball game creates a synergy with its fans by encouraging them to bring their cameras to games, which began with increasingly regularity in the late 1940s and early 1950s. Teams would designate a specific day when fans would be invited to photograph their favorite players. This promotion became known widely as "Photo Day" or "Camera Day" and remains popular. The rhythms of the game-day experience provide fans with the opportunity to snap a photograph prior to that first pitch, during the action, and then after the last out of the game is recorded. These snapshots create a timeless record of a fan's ballpark experience. The subject matter could be a ballpark, a player entering the facility, a player signing autographs during batting practice, or perhaps long after the game's conclusion when a fan engages a player quite by accident in a place of public accommodation.

VERY CAMP. At 14 years old, I attended Ted Williams Baseball Camp in Lakeville, Massachusetts. Ted was there every day and often gave one-on-one instruction to the campers. I had not gotten a hit in my first 14 at-bats and was struggling. Ted took me to the batting cages and fed the pitching machine while giving me instructions on how to hit. It was just Ted and I. I wound up hitting .320 that summer and made the camp All-Star team. (Author's collection.)

PARK AT THE PARK. Buzzie Bavasi was the Padres president when I joined the Padres, and one smart car dealer custom painted a car that we called the "Buzzie Buggy." Each employee had the opportunity to drive it for a week during the season, and then we gave it to a lucky fan on Fan Appreciation Day. This one was given away in 1976. (Author's collection.)

One

TALKING BASEBALL

In 1975, when I would correspond with my parents about my job and fledgling career in baseball, the shared highlight was getting to work with Jerry Coleman. As I was growing up in New York, Jerry's career as the Yankees' second baseman was winding down. He then became a broadcaster for the "Bronx Bombers." Many times our playground ball games were announced in Coleman style: "Strasberg got a hold of that one, folks, it's heading to the wall. It's gone. Home run."

One of the preeminent presents I received for my 14th birthday was a small, imported reel-to-reel tape recorder. I could tape the radio broadcasts by putting the microphone in front of the speaker and then emulate Jerry weaving his accounts of games. During one hot summer day game at Yankee Stadium when I was 14 years old, I snuck up to the seats behind the WPIX broadcast booth, called out "Mr. Coleman," and motioned to throw him a baseball to autograph. He gestured to me to throw him the ball and asked, "Why me?" The only words that came to my lips were also what I truly felt, "Because you are the great Jerry Coleman."

Jerry is truly one of the most self-effacing men I have ever known. When I was on the job for a week or two with the Padres, I caught Jerry in a moment of relaxation and shared with him that I still had the autographed ball and all his baseball cards from the 1950s. Gaining confidence by the moment, I asked if he had anything else that I could add to my Coleman collection. Without hesitating, Jerry took off his watch and handed to me. I stammered that I could not take something so expensive and personal. With that, he took out his money clip and started to hand it to me. The same response ensued, but I added, "Besides, it's personal, and how would people know it came from you?" Jerry then took out a pen, folded a dollar bill into the clip, and signed the dollar bill with "This is my dollar. Jerry Coleman." I still have both.

Once I was hired, Jerry alone did more for my Padres career than anyone and more than I could have imagined. My name was regularly mentioned in his radio broadcasts, and he had me answer fan mail trivia questions after each home game in a segment called "Ask Andy." The fan response was not great initially, so I used the Woody Allen approach and wrote my own fan mail complete with questions for about three weeks before the segment caught on.

Had it not been for Jerry repeatedly mentioning my name on the air, who knows what may have happened? Through him, I had instant credibility and name recognition when I was doing all I could to sell Padres season tickets to fans.

Perhaps it was hero worship, I am not sure; I so admired Jerry and his devotion to family and holiday gatherings that during the tail end of the 1975 season I must have hinted for an invite to Thanksgiving dinner at his home no less than two dozen times. When I did not secure an invite, I finally in my unmistakable pushy way asked him directly if I could join his family. "Why of course, Andy, I'm glad you reminded me." And it was a lovely time.

Years later, making amends for my perceived blunders and lapses of etiquette, I apologized to Jerry for being so obnoxious at the time. The response was a classic Coleman, "Andy, I don't even remember last Thanksgiving and what we had for dinner. Don't worry about it"—ever the gracious gentleman, Mr. Jerry Coleman.

During Jerry's Yankee career, his uniform number was 42. At the same time, the Dodgers' 42 was worn by Jackie Robinson. Soon after Jerry passed away in January 2014, I couldn't help but think about a Jackie Robinson quote that I had read years ago, "A life is not important except in the impact it has on other lives." Jackie could have had Jerry in mind when he was quoted, because since his passing I am amazed at the impact Jerry has had on so many lives—fortunately I am one of them.

THE COLONEL. "The voice of the San Diego Padres," Jerry Coleman was awarded the Ford C. Frick Award for his major contributions to baseball as a broadcaster by the National Baseball Hall of Fame in 2005. The award is given annually and was named after the former commissioner of baseball. Jerry had also broadcast games for the New York Yankees after his playing career and nationally on CBS Radio. Coleman would often say "Oh Doctor" when doing a broadcast and credits his former Yankee manager, Casey Stengel, as the major influence of using that term, as Stengel always referred to everyone as doctor. (Jan Brooks.)

WISH UPON A STAR. Dave Sniff was the KFMB Radio producer and engineer for Padres radio games for many years. Although not part of his duties, Sniff gladly accepted the responsibility for throwing out the star during the broadcast when Jerry Coleman would exclaim one of his trademark calls, "You can hang a star on that one," when there was an exceptional play during the game. Coleman explained that it came about as a reference to his childhood school days when, if you did something great in class, the teacher would put a gold star on your paper as a reward. (Tom Larwin.)

MR. PERSONALITY. Ted Leitner brought his broadcasting shtick to San Diego in 1978 and was immediately a hit with the fans and one of the most popular personalities in San Diego. It was obvious from the moment he opened his mouth that Ted had a lot of personality to share with his audience doing television as a sports anchor on CBS TV 8 and radio broadcasts on KFMB Radio. Throughout his career, Leitner has always made himself available for Madres lunches. His ability to talk about the team with sincerity, honesty, and a sense of humor is refreshing and entertaining. Ted has never forgotten that deep down inside he's still a 12-year-old fan who loves baseball. (Madres.)

CUE LESS. Ted Leitner's charm and knowledge were transmitted through the local television cameras without the use of cue cards or a teleprompter, which in effect separated him from all other sports broadcasters on TV. When talking to his audience, Ted never sugarcoated a play, player, manager, or anything else that came to his mind during a broadcast, which has kept him on-air since 1980. (Don Dewolf.)

BROADCAST BLEACHER CREATURES. To help stimulate ticket sales for the bleachers on day games at San Diego Stadium in the late 1970s, the Padres' radio crew would broadcast from the left-field bleachers. Producer Tommy Jorgenson and broadcasters Jerry Coleman and shirtless Dave Campbell are in the left-field bleachers under the sun and calling the action. The Padres renamed the seating area the "Fan Tan Section" and sold sun-protection cream called Fantan cream. (Tom Walsh.)

MONDAY, MONDAY. Possessing experience as a result of his 19 years playing major-league baseball, as well as being blessed with a great voice, Rick Monday was destined for mic stardom. Just like the players, broadcasters have to hone their skills during spring training. Rick looks at his scorecard during a short break at a spring training game in Yuma, Arizona. (Larry Carpa.)

INFINITY. The Padres drafted John Kruk in 1981 and brought him up through their minor-league system. When Kruk made his debut with the team in 1986, he wore no. 44 before switching to no. 8. When John was asked for the reason of the number change, his answer was thought provoking and profound, "Because when I slide into second base, my number changes from eight to infinity." Kruk played for the Padres until 1989, when he was traded to the Phillies. He is best remembered in San Diego for being the back end of the first group of players to hit back-to-back-to-back home runs to start a game during the Padres' home opener in 1987, following Marvell Wynne and Tony Gwynn in the lineup. Unfortunately, the Padres lost to the San Francisco Giants 13-6. Kruk is now working for ESPN as analyst, broadcaster, and philosopher. (Madres.)

HONDO, THE WIZ, AND FAST EDDIE. The Padres needed to replace Jerry Coleman in the broadcaster's booth in 1980 when he went down to manage the team. They didn't have to look far. Eddie Doucette, a Poway resident, had a broadcasting resume that included working with many NBA teams, along with the Milwaukee Brewers, Cleveland Indians, and Houston Astros. Jerry Colangelo, who was the former owner of the Diamondbacks, was quoted as saying, "Doucette was one of the most creative broadcasters . . . an innovator, not an imitator. He informs, entertains, and is very knowledgeable. He's the whole package." Prior to the 1981 season, new Padres manager Frank Howard and Eddie Doucette (in sunglasses) bookend shortstop Ozzie Smith at the Junior Padres caravan autograph table. The three gentlemen were regular guest attractions for the Friday-night or Saturday-afternoon Padres caravan stops at shopping malls throughout the county. Fans could chat with Padres personnel or get an autograph as they did here in the Mira Mesa shopping center. (Lucy Dickson.)

THE DUKE OF SAN DIEGO. In 1969, the Padres' first year in the National League, one of their marquee names was former Dodger and Fallbrook resident Duke Snider. "The Duke" filled many roles for the Padres that year. He provided color commentary for Padres radio and television broadcasts and was the Padres' batting instructor during that first spring training. Duke's friendship with then–Padres president Buzzie Bavasi went back many years to those Dodger days in Brooklyn. My dad, Dennis, worked at the stadium in a variety of capacities for the Pads and had the opportunity to have his picture taken with this baseball legend. (Tom Walsh.)

Mmmmm Good. Dave "Soupy" Campbell began his major-league career as a middle infielder for the Detroit Tigers in 1967. Soupy also played for the Padres (1970–1973), the St. Louis Cardinals (1973), and the Houston Astros (1973–1974). After his playing career, Campbell would attend Padres games, sitting in the upper deck by himself and practicing his ability to do the play by play of a baseball game. Dave worked for a local San Diego radio and television station and then in 1977 went back on the field, this time as the manager of the 1977 Amarillo Gold Sox of the Texas League. His team finished in last place that year, which probably convinced him in 1978 to move to the Padres' broadcast booth, where he teamed up with Jerry Coleman. (Madres.)

Forever Plaid. Homegrown broadcaster Bob Chandler is personable and knowledgeable. He graduated with a radio and television degree from San Diego State University. His uncanny ability to instantaneously recall information or provide statistical data has given Padres fans years of listening pleasure. Here, Bob is wearing a checkered sport coat and is about to talk to Padres pitcher Dan Spillner at a Madres luncheon. (Madres.)

15

VALENTINE'S DAY. After his playing career ended in 1979, Bobby Valentine, who had played for the Padres in 1975, 1976, and 1977, began working for ESPN, which at the time was a start-up network that had a crazy idea of devoting all of its programming exclusively to sports. I was walking through the Otesaga Hotel in Cooperstown, New York, in 1980, and I spotted Mets broadcaster Ralph Kiner chatting with Bobby. Kiner was the Pacific Coast League Padres general manager for a while after his playing career, before he worked for the Mets. (Rob Johnson.)

THE HALL CALLS. In 2005, Jerry Coleman, his wife Maggie, and their daughter Chelsea are seen having breakfast in the famous Otesaga Hotel the morning he was to receive the Ford C. Frick Award in Cooperstown, New York. (Rob Johnson.)

16

POKER FACE. MLB Network's in-studio host and play-by-play announcer Matt Vasgersian broadcast Padres games for seven seasons. It was during his time in San Diego that he began his annual charity, a Texas Hold 'Em tournament benefitting Tender Loving Canines Assistance Dogs in Solana Beach and the San Diego County Fallen Officers Fund. (Madres.)

HAAAAAAY LAAAADY. Jerry Coleman's longtime friend and movie legend Jerry Lewis would on occasion stop by and catch a Padres game from the broadcast booth. Lewis met Coleman in the early 1950s, when they were both in New York. Ted Leitner still to this day can't get over the fact that he met Jerry Lewis. Watching and enjoying Jerry Lewis visiting with Ted is author Andy Strasberg. (Author's collection.)

IN A PINCH. The affable former pinch-hitter Mark Sweeney, who played for seven major-league teams and starred with the Padres on three different occasions (1997–1998, 2002, and 2005), is now a Fox Sports San Diego studio analyst. (Madres.)

HAIR YOU ARE. Mark Grant has been a baseball broadcaster for the Padres since 1997. His insights on games and pop culture are unmatched in the Padres' broadcast booth. He was a major-league pitcher from 1984 to 1993 and was part of the Padres' pitching staff from 1987 to 1990. Here is "Mud" (a nickname given to him by San Francisco Giants coach Danny Ozark in reference to the pitcher Jim "Mudcat" Grant, who pitched in the big leagues from 1958 to 1971) answering questions at a Madres lunch during his Padres pitching days with those trademark dimples and when he had hair. (Madres.)

Two

OUT OF THE PARK

Some of my early Padres experiences involved accompanying players to personal appearances for a six-week stretch during the offseason, typically to a shopping center within the county. Our Padres caravans would make the trek on Friday nights and Saturdays, when the malls were most crowded. Players would be scheduled to sign autographs for two hours, and I would try to sell Junior Padres tickets to kids 14 and younger.

Often, the initial wave of kids was expended in the first half hour of signature signing. I then started holding free drawings for Padres items as an incentive to the kids to stick around. Small mic in hand, I would encourage the youngsters to become a member of the Junior Padres for only $1, which would entitle them to 11 tickets for admission to games. I also conducted a free raffle drawing at each location. Fans simply completed an entry form with name, age, and address, with the condition that they must be present in order to win. Ballplayers often have a warped sense of humor. When they have too much spare time on their hands, practical jokes become the norm rather than the exception—I never saw it coming.

I took my responsibilities seriously and was trying to do the best job I could. I alternated having players reach in to pull out a winning entry. After the first winner was announced, I was handed the next slip and read the name of the next one. After one prize had been claimed on a cool January evening, the next winner was announced as "Sue Perman. Is Sue Perman here? Remember you must be present to win . . . Sue Perman?" One of the players leaned over to me and in a voice that sounded kind and solicitous suggested I was perhaps not saying the name with the right pronunciation. Try saying the name faster, as if it were one word and not two, he suggested. Anxious to please, I followed the player's advice and said, "OK, the winner is Superman." As if on cue, the three Padres players exploded in hee-haw laughter. I thought I had learned my lesson and would now be more alert during later caravans. In fact, the next day I was handed a blank entry except for the name Dick Hertz, but I showed them that they couldn't make a fool out of me twice. Unfortunately, the players patiently outwaited me, and about three weeks later I was had again, this time with a different name but the same results: "And, the winner is . . . Chuck Roast."

Another memorable experience involved Ozzie Smith. Just prior to opening the gates of San Diego Stadium during the early part of the Padres 1978 season, I noticed our rookie sensation at shortstop do a standing back flip in foul territory. I eventually asked Ozzie if he would consider adding some zest to Padres Fan Appreciation Day as a little bonus entertainment. Ever the reserved man, Ozzie demurred with concern that he would be seen as showboating. One of the veterans on the team, Gene Tenace, talked him into it. Gene's daughter had seen the flip and told her dad about "how cool it was," and Gene in turn convinced Ozzie to give fans a treat.

It was a long season that saw the Padres finish in fourth place. On October 1, during Fan Appreciation Day, Ozzie took his position to start the game and did the back flip. The fans went nuts. The Padres beat the Dodgers 4-3 in 11 innings on an Oscar Gamble single that scored Dave Winfield. Ozzie went 0-4, but in the eyes of the fans, he was the star of the game.

There are fans with dubious memories who will avow Ozzie did that flip before every Padres game—not true. The man who would play his way into enshrinement at Cooperstown in 2002 reserved his signature flip for opening day, the final day of the season, and eventually post-season games when he played for the St. Louis Cardinals. And I saw the first one . . . and the last one.

JOLTIN'. Joe DiMaggio stops to pose for a photograph with Don Smith of El Cajon while playing in a golf tournament. Joe D. responded to Don's question as to how's it going with, "Good and not so good." Joe explained, "Unfortunately, I can't go anywhere without being recognized, and as a result, no matter where I go, I order room service, and I have my dinner in my room. I guess it's great to be recognized, but I'm limited in what I can do and where I can go." Beginning in 1969, DiMaggio was always introduced as the greatest living major-league baseball player. (Don Smith.)

RELAXED. During the offseason, after his Triple Crown season leading the 1967 Boston Red Sox to the World Series, Carl Yastrzemski is being interviewed by NBC broadcaster Joe Garagiola before he tees off at the La Costa Resort in California. (Paul Joba.)

OFFSEASON. In the 1970s, San Diego Padres caravans began in mid-January on Friday evenings and Saturday afternoons. The caravans took place at shopping centers around the county. Ven in San Diego, many times the Friday evenings were chilly. Pictured are, from left to right, outfielder Johnny Grubb, broadcasters Bob Chandler and Jerry Coleman, and Padres ace Randy Jones, looking to sign autographs and keep warm at the Grossmont Shopping Center on a Friday night in January 1975. (Author's collection.)

A TIP OF THE CAP. The best thing the 1969 Padres had going for them was the fact other National League teams would be playing in Mission Valley. San Diego baseball fans who wanted to enjoy major-league baseball no longer had to travel to Anaheim to catch the Angels or Los Angeles to watch the Dodgers. The Padres' front office realized what they were selling and used the caps of Willie Mays, Hank Aaron, Roberto Clemente, Ernie Banks, Ron Santo, Pete Rose, and Tom Seaver on their billboards promoting season tickets. (Linda Shaw.)

HAY PADRES. The concept of taking the Padres' team photograph at a popular San Diego tourist attraction naturally turned to the zoo in 1979. I received a little bit of push back from some of the players, but for the most part the team got a kick out of visiting the San Diego Zoo. The players were to sit on bales of hay in front of the elephant exhibit. The out-of-town visitors who just happened to be at the zoo on that day were surprised when the team showed up unannounced. Everything went smoothly until the next day, when I heard that one of the elephants that was in the photograph died unexpectedly. It must have been a Dodgers fan. Can you spot Rollie Fingers, Ozzie Smith, and Dave Winfield in this candid photograph? (Author's collection.)

ON A MISSION. The first Padres team photograph taken outside of San Diego Stadium was across the street at the San Diego Mission in 1978. Rollie Fingers expressed his unhappiness by subtly pulling out a magazine appropriately titled *Mad* to make his point. (Author's collection.)

ALL ABOARD. The 1981 team photograph was to be shot at the *Star of India*, and the players started to emerge from the clubhouse and slowly head out into the parking lot. They were not thrilled to be taken out of their "normal routine" to take a team photograph, but they were getting accustomed to it. Padres coach Whitey Wietelmann quickly realized that he would provide the transportation from the stadium to the bus, and in this photograph he is transporting Padres manager Frank Howard. (Author's collection.)

STATUESQUE. As they arrived in San Diego for the 1992 All-Star Game, fans found a living baseball player "statue" striking a pose at the luggage carousel at Lindbergh Field. I took photographs because I knew these would be keepsakes for my buddies some day. (Joe Buenavista.)

TAKE OFF. I was fresh out of the Navy when I volunteered to be a part of the San Diego community that helped make the 1992 All-Star Game played at Jack Murphy Stadium a success. My responsibilities included a number of jobs, but the one I enjoyed the most was decorating the Lindbergh Airport Terminal. My purpose was to instill the excitement of the "Midsummer Classic" in San Diego. I might have gotten carried away, because I very delicately placed a Padres all-star cap on the heads of the *Charles A. Lindbergh: The Boy and the Man* statue by Paul T. Granlund. (Joe Buenavista.)

23

CAMERA ACTION. During the taping of a baseball instructional video, once the live pitching started I took cover and shot this photograph of Tony while standing safely behind all the lights and cameras. (Doug Heron.)

NO PEPPER. Tony Gwynn was at the University of California–Riverside campus shooting a baseball video, and I had full access to shoot photographs. Note the "No Pepper" sign in the upper-left corner. I also thought it was very clever that at quick glance the uniform Tony was wearing resembled the design of the Padres at the time. (Doug Heron.)

GO SEE CAL. The Padres were filming a new TV commercial for T-shirt night, and the location was behind the San Diego Stadium scoreboard in the parking lot. The San Diego Chicken and car dealer Cal Worthington play to the camera in this 1981 Padres commercial. (Author's collection.)

WIZARD OF AHHHS. Padres shortstop Ozzie Smith signs an autograph for a fan at the 1981 Mira Mesa Padres caravan Saturday stop. (Author's collection.)

BOOMER. Chris Berman (far left) of ESPN, along with John Saunders (far right), interview Padres players Fred McGriff (second from left) and Gary Sheffield (second from right) at a special party held in Balboa Park the night before the 1992 All-Star Game. Unfortunately, the American League beat up the National League, 13-6, and both Padres players were traded the next season. (Author's collection.)

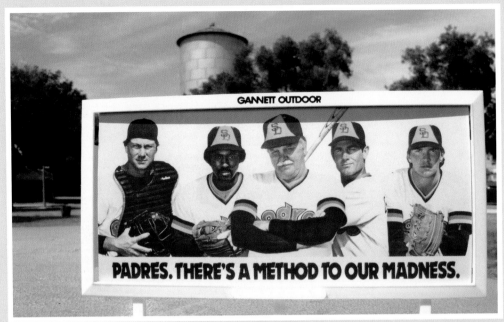

A SIGN OF THE TIMES. The Padres continued their advertising theme of madness with this billboard featuring, from left to right, Terry Kennedy, Garry Templeton, Dick Williams, Steve Garvey, and Tim Lollar. (Duane Dimock.)

HERE'S THE PITCH. The 7-Up Junior Padres Caravan & Clinic traveled around San Diego County to teach youngsters the proper way to play baseball. Padres catcher Terry Kennedy is on the microphone narrating what Padres coach Bob Cluck is doing in his batting stance. (Lucy Dickson.)

A Line Drive. Tony Gwynn is deserving of all the accolades, honors, and admiration he receives from the San Diego community. The fact that during his hall-of-fame baseball career he opted to stay in San Diego and play for the Padres rather than seek millions of dollars more in other cities is a testament to the kind of person he is. As time passes, his on-field accomplishments will grow in stature, not only among knowledgeable baseball fans but also for those of us who enjoyed his Padres years—we are the fortunate ones. (Fred O. Rodgers.)

It Suits Them. The Padres in 1985 were invited to every imaginable event during the offseason. Here are, from left to right, Terry Kennedy, Steve Garvey, Dave Dravecky, and Tim Flannery in black tie, along with Padres president Ballard Smith. (Madres.)

ON THE MOVE. Throughout Tony Gwynn's San Diego Padres career, many fans climbed aboard the bandwagon to root for the future Baseball Hall of Famer. The local San Diego Mass Transit Corporation decorated a bus with Tony Gwynn's image during the year he collected his 3,000th hit (August 6, 1999). From left to right are Ron Yagura, Gwynn, and Tom Larwin. (Tom Larwin.)

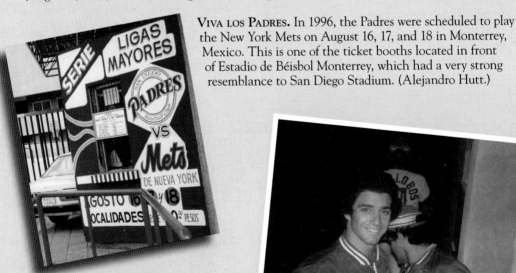

VIVA LOS PADRES. In 1996, the Padres were scheduled to play the New York Mets on August 16, 17, and 18 in Monterrey, Mexico. This is one of the ticket booths located in front of Estadio de Béisbol Monterrey, which had a very strong resemblance to San Diego Stadium. (Alejandro Hutt.)

BÉISBOL. John D'Acquisto, a hard-throwing right-hander who had a 10-year career in major-league baseball, grew up in San Diego and played at one time for the San Diego Padres and for Los Potros de Tijuana in the winter. This snapshot of him was taken on November 12, 1977. (Madres.)

YANKEES AND WHITE SOX. While Padres fans were comfortably seated at PETCO Park to take in a rare Yankees-Padres game on Saturday, August 3, 2013, I was enjoying the same contest from the comfort of my New York apartment living room while also contemplating whether I might be needing some new socks soon. I was asleep two minutes and eight seconds after the last pitch (good job, Mariano)—Padres fans, not so soon. (Marty Appel.)

TWO RIGHTS. The relationship between a baseball player and a fan can be mutually beneficial if it's the right fan and the right player. The Padres' Mark Sweeney was a featured speaker at a Madres luncheon in 2002. One of his biggest fans was Dee Anderson, who had recently moved to a convalescent home and was recovering from a stroke. At one point, Mark was kind enough to stop and visit with Dee, and as a result of that meeting he would visit her once a month until he had to report to spring training. Mark kept up the friendship and made it a point that even when he was no longer on the Padres he would make arrangements when his new team was in town to play at PETCO for Dee to come on the field during batting practice to visit. When Dee passed away, Mark said that it was like losing a favorite grandmother. (Madres.)

SMILING GOOSE. The 2010 Baseball Cooperstown Parade featured all attending Hall of Famers, and that year there were almost 50 who participated. Here's "Goose" Gossage, who was a key figure for the Padres in 1984 when they went to the World Series. (Louise and Dave Cavallin.)

ROUNDTRIPPER. Jerry Coleman strikes a batting pose during a lull at a 1976 Padres caravan. Jerry loved to talk about the fact that he hit 16 career home runs while playing for the Yankees, and the only time a photograph of him hitting a homer was in a newspaper, the caption misidentified him. (Author's collection.)

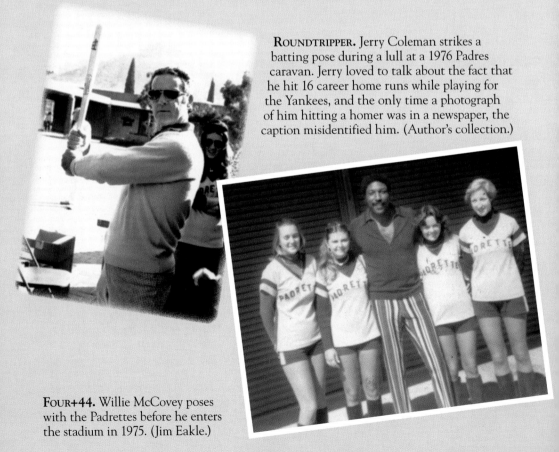

FOUR+44. Willie McCovey poses with the Padrettes before he enters the stadium in 1975. (Jim Eakle.)

Three

TWO STORIES TALL

Among the many bright and personable college students hired by the Padres to staff the ticket office during a baseball season was a special one, Amanda Sperry. Soon after meeting Amanda, Patti and I asked her to consider being our dog sitter. Other girls were similarly enlisted, but on Amanda's rotation we always returned to a happy dog; Amanda also seized the opportunity to spend some quality time with her boyfriend, Gary.

Apparently Patti and I helped Cupid's aim, because on one of our trips out of town, Gary asked Amanda to marry him. Patti and I attended the wedding of the couple, and in a few short years Amanda gave birth to a baby boy. As a unique gift, I sent the already proud parents a genuine National League player contract for their newborn son. It was signed by the president of the Padres as well as the commissioner of baseball, Bowie Kuhn. The contract made their son a Padre for life with an accompanying symbolic and ceremonial salary of $1. Gary and Amanda had the contract framed, and it was hung proudly in their son's bedroom.

As fate would have it, the youngest Padres signee had a great high school career as a pitcher, good enough to be selected in the first round of the 2002 major-league draft by the Philadelphia Phillies, with whom he ultimately inked a far more substantial contract than the one I obtained for him 18 years earlier. You can imagine my great joy and satisfaction watching Amanda and Gary's son, Cole Hamels, make his impressive mark in the major leagues since 2006.

Another story starts while waiting patiently in line at the concession stand at the 1979 All-Star game in Seattle. I overheard a young man in the equally snail-paced line next to me say that he was traveling around the country that summer, from ballpark to ballpark, seeing as many games as he could. He struck a chord with me in his Yankees cap and looked to be in his early 20s, kind of a retro version of myself and with the same passion for seeing the game played.

I had a short debate with myself and decided to "big league" the young man and handed him one of my Padres business cards. He looked at it, and I said, "If you haven't been to San Diego yet and want to see a Padres game, you can be my guest." From the expression on his face, you would have thought I just offered him a lifetime pass. I assured him I was not kidding and told him he could bring the two guys with whom he was traveling.

Nearly two weeks later, I got a call from my concession-line friend saying that he was going to make it to San Diego in a couple of days and wanted to know if the offer was still good. I told him "absolutely" and left three tickets at will call under his name. During the game, I made my way down to the seats and within a few moments learned he was from New Jersey, was a schoolteacher, and loved baseball.

The young man and I kept in touch over the winter, and the following season I invited him to be my guest at a Padres game if he visited San Diego. I also mentioned that the 1980 All-Star Game was going to be in Montreal and invited him to join me, my dad, and a friend if he was interested in attending the Midsummer Classic. "Of course," he shouted, and we all had a great time driving up to the game from New York City. Our friendship continued to grow, and at one point a few years later my Jersey pal shared with me that he was going to quit his job as a schoolteacher and get into baseball. I immediately wondered if I had helped ruin this young man's life. I quickly explained that working for a team is very stressful at times, had long hours, and could be filled with office politics. "Oh I don't want to work for a team," he explained, "I want to be a major-league umpire."

Soon after, he left his teaching position and enrolled in an umpire school in Florida. After graduating, he was placed in the minor leagues and worked in the New York–Penn League, Carolina League, South Atlantic League, Southern League, Triple-A Alliance, International League, American Association, Florida State League, and Eastern League. It did not matter to me what league he was in, as I was proud of someone who followed his dream. Then, on June 4, 1991, twelve years after a random conversation in the concession line at the Kingdome, I received a call that my Jersey pal was going to the majors for a week to assume a relief spot for an umpire who was taking an in-season vacation.

The aspiring umpire told me that he would be working first base in St. Louis for his first major-league assignment, with the Cardinals hosting the Dodgers. Without his knowledge, I hired a local photographer to shoot the game and focus solely on the umpire at first base. I told the photographer he had to arrive very early and be certain that he captured my friend's first official step on a major-league field. I also made arrangements for a bottle of celebratory champagne to be delivered to the umpires' dressing room after the game.

Over the next few years, and after a series of short call-ups, some disappointments, and frustrations, my buddy attained status as regular umpire and remains one of the unique group of 68 men who work major-league baseball games around the country. During the 2013 season, when his crew had a series in San Diego, I told him about my Fantography project and that I was looking for unique baseball photographs that have a San Diego theme. He asked me for an example, so I quickly explained, "You know, like you in street clothes, wearing your home plate umpire's mask, standing under the PETCO Park sign." Without a pause, he replied, "Let's do it." Thanks, Phil Cuzzi, for your dedication to baseball and even more so for our enduring friendship.

SAFE AT HOME. The ever-cooperating and congenial umpire Phil Cuzzi responds to a request for a most unusual snapshot at Petco Park in August 2013. (Author's collection.)

A GOOD-LOOKING PHILLIE. Teenager Amanda Sperry worked for the Padres from 1977 to 1982. Here, she reluctantly smiles for a snapshot request at a Padres picnic in 1978. (Lucy Dickson.)

Heavy Hitter. Teenage Amanda Sperry takes a cut during a Padres front-office softball game in the late 1970s. (Lucy Dickson.)

A Good Looking Pair of Genes. Cole Hamels met with his mom and dad for dinner during the season when the Phillies made a rare trip to play the Red Sox at Fenway Park in 2012. (Author's collection.)

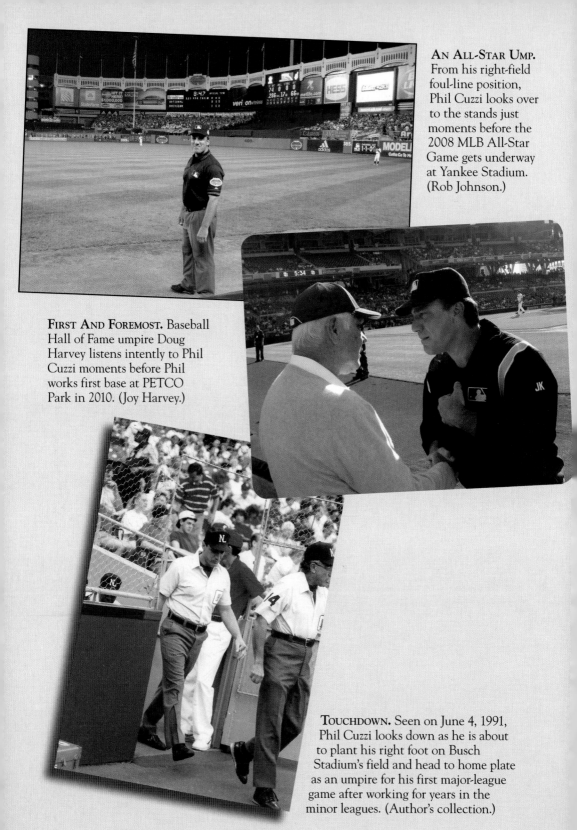

AN ALL-STAR UMP. From his right-field foul-line position, Phil Cuzzi looks over to the stands just moments before the 2008 MLB All-Star Game gets underway at Yankee Stadium. (Rob Johnson.)

FIRST AND FOREMOST. Baseball Hall of Fame umpire Doug Harvey listens intently to Phil Cuzzi moments before Phil works first base at PETCO Park in 2010. (Joy Harvey.)

TOUCHDOWN. Seen on June 4, 1991, Phil Cuzzi looks down as he is about to plant his right foot on Busch Stadium's field and head to home plate as an umpire for his first major-league game after working for years in the minor leagues. (Author's collection.)

Four

PERFECT EXPOSURE

One of the more difficult challenges confronting me as the Padres promotions director was not unlike dealing with an unruly teenager. Getting the players to do something that took them out of their normal routine was akin to expecting them to pick up the debris in the dugout or clean the clubhouse after a game. Traditions often come in pairs. For instance, the tradition of Camera Day is typically accompanied by the tradition of the players deciding they will not cooperate. One Sunday in 1978, two hours before Camera Day festivities were to begin, I was summoned via phone by team manager Roger Craig to come to his office on the double. Roger knew my apprehension about players mugging for the camera, and when he called he said in his inimitably slow, friendly, Southern drawl, "You better get down here, Andy, cause we've got a problem." I said, "I'll be right there" and hung up without another word. *Now what* I thought en route to see the club's skipper. As I burst into the office, Roger was sitting at his desk and motioned me to close the door. I was waiting for the bombshell. "Andy, the players have voted not to take the field for Camera Day. Not one of them will go along with it." I sat down in disbelief. I could barely utter "why?" and Roger responded, "Because of you, Andy, they just don't like you." I was crushed. "Roger, are you sure? This can't be happening."

A big old grin started to expand its way across Roger's face as he reached into his desk drawer. "Yeah, Andy, I'm just kidding you." And with a flip of his wrist, he sent a cap flying in my direction. Oh my gosh, it was a Dodgers cap Roger had worn when he pitched for Brooklyn back in 1956. "Here's the cap I promised you." From being near tears a minute earlier, I was now the one grinning while holding Roger's game-used Dodgers cap from one of the most famous teams of baseball's golden era.

Ozzie Smith
1979

WE'RE OFF TO SEE THE WIZARD. Padres players had a special picnic party for the Junior Padres in the summer of 1979. The party took place under the scoreboard in right field of San Diego Stadium. The players served ice cream and soda. It was so easy to pose my kids, Laurie and Tom Jr., with Ozzie Smith, who was in his second year of major-league baseball. (Tom Larwin.)

THE BROCKABRELLA. One of the most popular postgame promotions in the 1970s was "The Cash Scramble." Twenty fans were randomly selected from those in attendance, and when the game immediately ended they were escorted down onto the field. Scattered all over the infield were $10,000 in $1, $5, and $10 bills. Fans were given 90 seconds to pick up as many bills as they could. As the starting pistol went off to begin the Padres' 1978 cash scramble, Jay Johnstone (wearing an umbrella hat called a "Brockabrella" in this photograph), who everyone thought was in the Padres clubhouse taking a shower, ran out from the Padres dugout and, along with the fans, competitively began scooping up money to the laughter and applause of Padres fans in the stands. Padres catcher Gene Tenace is to the left of Jay. (Madres.)

FIELDING REQUESTS. When the Padres played at Lane Field, there were occasional opportunities to go on the field and get pictures of the players and their autographs. This was an especially crazy time, because I didn't know which player to start with many times. Here's my snapshot of Dick Faber, who played for the Padres in 1953. (Jack and Susie Nopal.)

FLANSTER. Jerry Royster and Tim Flannery shared playing time at second base for the 1985 Padres, and the two complemented each other perfectly. Royster played 80 games at second and Flannery 126 games at the same position; many times one would finish the game that the other started. Their combined their totals that year were 71 RBIs and 178 hits. For Camera Day, they switched jerseys to the delight of fans who brought their cameras. (Madres.)

LOST IN TRANSLATION. Bob Owchinko pitched for the Padres from 1976 to 1979. In 1978, our son Tom Jr. had his picture taken with him. Japanese television broadcasters that year had to change Owchinko's name to Bob Smith when the Padres played a pre-season game in Hawaii against the Yakult Swallows because *owchinko* means "little penis" in Japanese. (Tom Larwin.)

THE VIEW. During the Padres' Camera Day, fans were permitted to go on the field and take snapshots of the players. The infield dirt was absolutely off limits, as you can see in this photograph taken from the plaza-level walkway. Fans could sit in the stadium and look out at the hills behind the scoreboard. It was so peaceful. (Madres.)

FUNNY NOSE AND GLASSES. During the Padres' 1992 Camera Day, a couple of players (Bruce Hurst, left, and Larry Andersen, right) were disguised as 12-year-olds in major-league uniforms. They were "boys being boys" no matter how old or how talented. (Larry Carpa.)

GOLDEN. Cito Gaston played for the Padres from 1969 to 1974. Clarence Edwin Gaston grew up wanting to be a truck driver, a singer, or major-league baseball player. "Cito," as he was known, received his nickname due to a resemblance to a Mexican wrestler. Gaston won two batting titles playing winter baseball in Venezuela and had Hank Aaron for a roommate while playing for the Braves. Cito has been quoted giving credit to Aaron for teaching him "how to be a man; how to stand on my own." Canada will long remember Gaston, as he was the first African American manager in major-league history to win a World Series when he was the pilot of the Toronto Blue Jays in 1992; they repeated as champs in 1993. (Betty Armstrong.)

HOMETOWN BASEBALL MAN. Dave Garcia lived in El Cajon during a baseball career that included almost 20 years as an infielder in the minor leagues. He began managing in the minors at the age of 27 in 1948 for the New York Giants. In 1969, Dave was one of the managers in the Padres farm system before becoming the major-league third-base coach for the Padres from 1970 to 1973. Garcia was a coach for the Indians and Angels and eventually became the manager for each team. He also spent time working for the Milwaukee Brewers, Kansas City Royals, and Colorado Rockies and can nowadays be seen sitting behind home plate at almost every Padres game. (Val Schiller.)

BUSTED. This photograph documents two very interesting things. The first is that on some Padres Camera Day promotions, the visiting team was invited to participate. As you can see, the Cincinnati Reds are on the field chatting with Padres outfielder Gene Locklear, who played one season in 1973 for the Reds. There is a rule (3.09) in major-league baseball about how players of opposing teams shall not fraternize at any time while in uniform. It also states, "They are also forbidden from mingling with or addressing spectators." (Val Schiller.)

No. 11. One of the most popular Padres in the 1970s was Enzo Hernandez. His popularity had little to do with playing ability. In large part, fans liked Enzo because of the way Padres public address announcer John DeMott would identify him in the lineup. DeMott would run Enzo's uniform number and name as if it was one word, "And playing shortstop for the Padres, Numberelevenenzonhernandez." (Madres.)

HARRY AND MINNIE. Harry Simpson (background) and Minnie Minoso over to the stands at Lane Field so fans could get an autograph or snap a photograph. Minoso played for the PCL Padres in 1949 and 1950. He is the only man to have played professionally in seven decades and is also the last major-leaguer from the 1940s to play in a major-league game. Minnie was baptized Saturnino Orestes Arrieta Armas in Cuba. He received the nickname "Minnie" when he was in the waiting room of a dentist and thought that when the name Minnie was called, it was for him. Minoso is also known as the "Cuban Comet." While with the White Sox, Minnie had the distinction of getting hit with a pitch and homering in the same at bat. He crowded the plate as he usually did and turned into a pitch so he would get hit and take first base. The home plate ump didn't allow it, and the at-bat continued. He then connected with a pitch for a home run. Notably, Minoso was one of the original nine players to receive a Rawlings Gold Glove when the award began in 1957. (Kay E. Scozzafava.)

GRUB HUG. My favorite player was Padres outfielder Johnny Grubb. He was a great hitter and fielder who knew he was my favorite. (Betty Armstrong.)

FOCUSED. What better time to shoot pictures of your favorite player than on Camera Day. Here is Johnny D'Acquisto getting into Camera Day just like the fans. (Lucy Dickson.)

SIGN HERE. In 1972, when Camera Day was scheduled, it was after Nate Colbert's amazing feat of hitting five homers in a doubleheader. Fans brought everything they could get their hands on to commemorate the accomplishment and have Nate autograph it. (Val Schiller.)

OH BROTHER. Robbie Alomar greets fans on the Padres' Camera Day early in his career. Robby and his brother Sandy Jr. played briefly for the Padres at the same time. Five pairs of brothers have played together for the Padres: Sandy and Roberto Alomar (1988–1989), Tony and Chris Gwynn (1996), Brian and Marcus Giles (2007), Adrian and Edgar Gonzalez (2008), and Jerry and Scott Hairston (2010). Only the Braves (nine), Pirates (eight), Giants (seven), Cardinals (seven), and Indians (six) have had more sets of brothers simultaneously on the roster. (Madres.)

NAME GAME. Steve Garvey gave one of the best quotes ever said by a player about other players: "The difference between the old ballplayer and the new ball player is the jersey. The old ballplayer cared about the name on the front. The new ballplayer cares about the name on the back." Some fans may also recall when Garvey showed up for his first Padres spring training in 1983, the company that makes the Padres' uniforms misspelled his name as "Gravey." (Madres.)

BAG MAN. Harry Simpson, an outfielder and first baseman, was one of the most popular minor-league Padres players. According to the 1951 *Cleveland Indians Sketch Book*, Simpson was called "Suitcase" by sportswriters after a comic-strip character in *Toonerville Folks*, which was also known as *Toonerville Trolley*. The reference was to Suitcase Simpson, who had feet the size of a suitcase. Harry's real nickname was "Goody," which came from his willingness to run errands and help neighbors in his hometown of Dalton, Georgia. (Kay E. Scozzafava.)

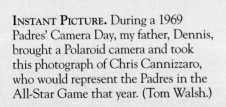

TOM HEART BASEBALL. My husband loves baseball, and Camera Day was one of his favorite promotions because he was able to go down on the field and take snapshots of the players. Naturally, I wanted a photograph of him on that day in 1984. (Kathy Larwin.)

INSTANT PICTURE. During a 1969 Padres' Camera Day, my father, Dennis, brought a Polaroid camera and took this photograph of Chris Cannizzaro, who would represent the Padres in the All-Star Game that year. (Tom Walsh.)

Whitey Wietelman

Lane Field - year - '49

IT'S CHILI. Long before Tony Gwynn was known as "Mr. Padre," Whitey Wietelmann had that distinction. Beginning in 1939, Whitey played for the Boston Braves for eight seasons, as well as 14 years in the minors, with four of those years as a member of the PCL Padres. Whitey stayed in San Diego after his active playing days and was a coach for the PCL Padres. He was then a coach for the Padres when they became a big-league club in 1969. Whitey was best known for being a "fix it kind of guy" and invented a baseball cleaner that was essentially a wooden box with large erasers in it that tumbled the baseballs to clean them up. Whitey's other claim to fame was his incredible chili that was known throughout the baseball world. Here, he is posing for the camera in 1949. (Kay E. Scozzafava.)

MY PAL BIG DAVE. Growing up, Dave Winfield was my favorite player. This photograph of us was taken around 1976 when I was 13 years old. Ed Runge, a former American League umpire who worked for the Padres on their speaker's bureau, was our next-door neighbor. Ed arranged for me to get down on the field before an old-timers game and have this snapshot taken. Later on, I saw Dave working out during the offseason at SDSU, and he played catch with me. He gave me a ride home, and I invited him into my house to see my Dave Winfield scrapbook. I remember he had a glass of orange juice, and I instructed my mom to "not to wash that glass." In the mid-1980s, I worked for Garvey Marketing Group, and Winfield became a client. When I applied to law school in 1991, he wrote a letter of recommendation. Since the late 1990s, I have represented Dave as his agent, and it has been one of the most rewarding professional and personal experiences of my life. (Randy Grossman.)

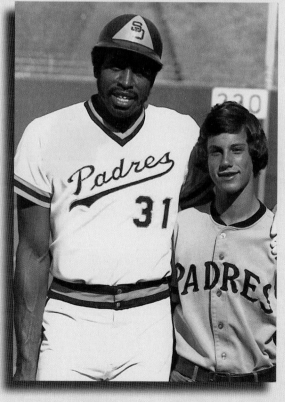

Five

PILOTS

Some of my most memorable times with the Padres were when I was on the field with the team during early batting practice before the gates opened to the general public. Sometimes, I had to apply a pinch to believe it was true. For a guy who did not make his high school varsity team, here I was fielding fly balls with major-leaguers. As with most other things in my life, I held firm to the belief that my passion and dedication would make up for and overshadow my lack of talent. On an eastern swing to play the Mets in my hometown, I summoned the courage to ask manager Dick Williams if I could work out with the team in Shea Stadium. To my surprise, Dick said yes, provided I wore a uniform that fit me.

When we reached New York, I called my dad and asked him to pick me up at noon at the team's hotel in midtown Manhattan, some seven hours before the first pitch of the night game. When we arrived at Shea around 12:45 p.m., my father accompanied me to the locker room, and I suited up in a Padres road uniform. Pause here for an observation about my enthusiasm. Here it is 1:30 p.m., and I am pacing the dugout, knowing the team bus will not depart the hotel until 5:00 p.m.

Around 3:00 p.m., several players came on the field for some extra practice. When the rest of the team arrived after 5:00 p.m., I joined Tim Flannery in the outfield for some catch to loosen our arms and shag a few flies as well. At one point, the players started verbally taking some shots at me and suggested I get some real action over at third base during batting practice. I walked slowly over to the grass behind third base and watched as baseballs were zooming off bats in my direction. I was probably well positioned for safety reasons in shallow left field, because several players kept telling me to "move in." I did, but I made sure only the toes of my cleats were on the infield dirt because I valued my nose and teeth. When the nonstop taunting finally found me with both feet planted on the infield dirt, a liner shot at me, and I had the presence of mind to stick out my glove and lean to my left, feel the smack of leather striking leather, and make the long throw across the diamond to first base. Armed with newly discovered courage, I then moved in another foot or two and caught a grounder in front of me. It was followed by a one-hopper to my right that I backhanded cleanly and threw to first. I could almost hear the cheers erupting from the crowd that was still awaiting the gates' opening. My abject fear had quickly turned to a measure of comfort and cockiness. I was, as the players say, "pickin' it."

After a few moments, I peeked into the dugout and recall being thrilled that my dad was able to share the experience. When batting practice ended and the players headed for the ramp to the clubhouse, I detoured to the dugout, where Dick Williams was sitting with my father. Positioning myself between them but leaning back far enough that my father could hear what Dick might say, I asked the skipper if he had seen me fielding those rockets at third base. "Yes, I did," he responded. I asked him what he thought of the job I did at third. Of course I was hoping he would say, "What the hell are you doing working in the front office" and suggest I begin a career on the field. Instead, I heard Dick ask, "Do you really want to know what I think?" "Yeah," I quickly said and leaned back to hear the anticipated praise. "Andy, I thought you looked a bit like a monkey on a leash trying to make love to a football."

I quickly turned to my father and said, "I'm done, let's go." We walked up the ramp into the visitors' clubhouse, where I showered and changed and did not utter a word until the third inning. The dream ended as quickly as it had begun. I was forced once more to live with the fact that I was not big-league material.

THE CURSE. Don Zimmer (left) was the Padres' second manager. He took over for Preston Gomez during the 1972 season and lasted until the end of the 1973 campaign. Nicknamed "Popeye," he and his wife, Soot, were married on August 16, 1951, at home plate while he was playing in the minors for the Brooklyn Dodgers organization. Zimmer was the Padres' manager when Padres pitcher Steve Arlin (right) was one strike away from a no-hitter. It was July 18, 1972, and they were facing the Phillies. With two outs in the ninth and two strikes on Phillies second baseman Denny Doyle, Padres rookie third baseman Dave Roberts looked in at Zimmer about where to position himself for the next pitch. Zimmer inexplicably had him in close to protect against the bunt. Doyle hit a one-hopper over Roberts's head, and Arlin's no hitter was history. Had Roberts not been playing in as Zimmer instructed, he would have easily caught the grounder and thrown him out. After the game, Arlin was icing his arm, and Zimmer walked up to him with a razor in hand, admitting his mistake, and told him to use it but to make it quick. To this day, Arlin gives Zimmer credit for the Padres never having a pitcher throw a no-hitter in their history and calls it "The Curse of Zimmer." Zimmer went on to manage the Red Sox (1976–1980), the Texas Rangers (1980–1982), and the Chicago Cubs (1988–1991). (Both, Betty Armstrong.)

STRIKE UP THE BAND. John McNamara was a catcher in the minor leagues and never played in the majors. After his playing days were over, John began a 10-year run of managing in the minors. McNamara got his big-league break as a manager in 1969 with the Oakland A's, when he replaced Hank Bauer with a couple of weeks left in the season. John then managed the A's for the entire 1970 season. He began managing the Padres in 1974. Coincidently, Padres fan Jim Eakle began an impromptu band of musicians that called themselves "McNamara's Band" that year. (Madres.)

THE DARK DAYS. Alvin Dark was the answer to the Padres' managing problems in 1977, following John McNamara's reign. Dark explained one of his theories for success in baseball by simply saying, "A fellow has to have faith in God above and Rollie Fingers in the bullpen." The end of Dark's days as Padres manager started to form at spring training in 1978. Alvin announced that Bill Almon was no longer the Padres' shortstop and that a minor-leaguer who had only played 68 games for Walla Walla in 1977 was going to be the full-time shortstop: Osborne Smith. Dark minimized the responsibilities of his coaching staff and didn't see eye to eye with some of his key veteran players. On March 21, 1978, the Padres fired their manager during spring training and gave Roger Craig the job. Padres owner Ray Kroc had the final say in the matter and was quoted in the *Sporting News* stating, "Alvin had a tendency to over manage." (Madres.)

DIFFERENT STROKES. When it was announced that Roger Craig was not being retained as Padres manager for the 1980 season and his replacement was going to be popular Padres broadcaster and former Yankee second baseman Jerry Coleman, many fans thought it was a prank of some sort. Some believed the new manager was Gary Coleman, the child actor who had just starred in the NBC made-for-TV movie *The Kid from Left Field*. The movie plot had Gary Coleman, who played J.R. Cooper, take over the team (the Padres) as manager. Jerry had agreed to try his hand as the team's skipper, but at the end of the season he had the option to return to the broadcaster's booth. He thought it was not in the Padres' best interest to keep the job as the club's pilot and decided to leave managing to someone else, attesting to the philosophy "different strokes for different folks." (Madres.)

HEAVE-HO. Steve Boros's tenure as a Padres manager is probably best remembered by one game that he didn't manage for the Padres. In the Padres-Braves game on Thursday June 5, 1986, at Jack Murphy Stadium, in the bottom of the third inning and no one out, Bip Roberts was on second base and Tony Gwynn was on first. Kevin McReynolds hit a comebacker to Braves pitcher Zane Smith, who threw to second base for one out and the relay to first to get McReynolds for the second out; meanwhile, Bip rounded third and tried to score as the Braves completed the double play. It appeared that Roberts slid around Ozzie Virgil's tag at the plate, but he was called out by home plate umpire Charlie Williams. The Padres' on-deck hitter, Steve Garvey, rushed up to home plate umpire Williams and verbalized his displeasure with the call and told Williams to "bear down." Those were the magic words according to Williams, who threw Garvey out of the game. It was the first time Garv had ever been thrown out of a major-league game. The next night, Padres manager Steve Boros arrived at home plate with the Padres line-up card and a videotape of the play from the previous night that showed Roberts had made it safely into home plate. Williams quickly realized what was happening and rather than accept the video as a gift, he gave Boros the "heave-ho" and threw him out before the game started. Boros lasted only one season (1986) as Padres manager. (Madres.)

A Bowa Constrictor. Larry Bowa was announced as the Padres' manager for the 1987 season. Storm Davis was acquired by the Padres before the 1987 season for Terry Kennedy and Mark Williamson. Davis had been very successful in Baltimore, going 61-43 with a 3.63 ERA over six seasons. Storm and Larry had a tempestuous relationship, as Larry expected Storm to help anchor the Padres rotation. Bowa and Davis weren't on the same page and feuded behind the scenes. Eventually, Bowa got so exasperated, he was quoted as saying, "Storm Davis thinks the 'SD' on our hat stands for Storm Davis." Davis was traded to Oakland on August 30. Bowa was gone not much later, as he did not survive a 19-30 start to the 1988 season. (Jan Brooks.)

Gentle Giant. No National League manager can claim to have finished in last place twice in the same season except for Frank Howard. During the strike-shortened 1981 season, it was decided that a winner would be declared for the first half before the strike and then a winner for the second half—the Padres were in the cellar for both. (Author's collection.)

Like a Monkey. Padres front-office executive Andy Strasberg would on occasion work out with the team. The uniform was real, but his playing abilities were suspect. (Belinda Bird.)

BROKEN CYCLE. Jim Riggleman piloted the Padres from 1992 to 1994, and while his record shows that he managed 291 games, there is one game he won but wishes he could do over again. The Padres were playing the Dodgers at Dodger Stadium on June 10, 1993, and by the fourth inning the Padres were ahead 4-0. After six innings, the lead had increased to 11-2. Tony Gwynn was having an incredible day at the plate. "T" hit a homer in the third inning, a double in the fifth inning, and a triple in the sixth inning, needing only a single to complete the cycle and become the first Padres player ever to accomplish the feat. Riggleman took Gwynn out of the game in the seventh inning and replaced him with Phil Clark, not realizing that the game's greatest single hitter only needed a single to complete the cycle. (Madres.)

WORLD SERIOUS. Dick Williams (left) was the first Padres manager to take the team to the World Series (1984). The key date of that memorable 1984 season many historians point to was August 12, 1984, when the Padres played the Braves in Atlanta. Atlanta's Pascual Pérez started the game by hitting Padres second baseman Alan Wigging with his first pitch. By the time the game was over, a total of 13 players had been thrown out of the game. Dick received a 10-day suspension and a $10,000 fine, but the "base brawl" fired up the Padres, and they continued their winning ways to capture the division. Williams was both admired and feared by his players. His seriousness about baseball fundamentals is legendary. Testimony from Tim Flannery, one of the most popular players on the team, perhaps best explains it: "I love Dick as a manager, but if I ever saw him when I'm through playing baseball, I'd run over him with my car." Here's a snapshot of Dennis Walsh, who, during Dick's tenure as manager, managed the Padres owner's box. It is interesting to note that Williams was the National League manager for the 1995 All-Star Game played in Minnesota and started five Padres players: Tony Gwynn, Steve Garvey, Graig Nettles, Terry Kennedy, and pitcher LaMarr Hoyt. The "Padres" beat the American League 6-1. (Tom Walsh.)

TRADER JACK. Jack McKeon was a career minor-leaguer who became a big-league manager and general manager. During the four years he was the Padres' general manager, "Trader Jack" moved 95 players. His personality was often describe by the media as a throwback to the "old school"—those days when baseball men smoked cigars, had a few drinks, and told with a great deal of animation colorful stories about the game. Jack was all that and more. For years, he was the face of the Padres organization regardless of the position held and always had time for fans. Making public appearances for sponsors came easy to Jack, who enjoyed being in the spotlight. During his time as manager, it was not unusual to see him stop by the local San Diego Toyota dealer's showroom in uniform on a weekend to have his photograph taken with fans like me. (Gary Holdinghausen.)

IF YOU KNEW SUSHI. Bruce Bochy is the first former player to have played for the Padres and managed it after his playing career. He began his managing career with the Padres in 1995, and it concluded after the 2006 season. During those 12 years, the Padres won 951 games, which gave Bochy the record for most wins during a manager's tenure in the club's history. In 1996, He established the record of managing a major-league baseball team in three countries (the United States, Canada, and Mexico). On a trip to Japan in November 2004, Bochy managed the MLB All-Stars when they played exhibition games against the Japanese All-Stars. During that trip, he is seen taking a break to have sushi at Kyubei, one of the best sushi bars in Japan, with noted baseball enthusiast and historian Fu-chan Fujisawa. (Fu-chan Fujisawa.)

Six

DOWN IN FRONT

I believe the era of the modern-day team mascots began in San Diego. Rick Leibert was then the program director for KGB-AM and FM radio stations and felt his stations would be more competitive in the marketplace with a mascot. Rick's choices were a frog and a chicken. Ultimately deciding on the chicken, Rick sought an interested radio intern from San Diego State University who would be willing to make personal appearances as the KGB Chicken for $2 an hour. The solicitation caught the eye of student Ted Giannoulas, and he became the persona of the chicken.

The first KGB promotional appearance for Ted was at the San Diego Zoo for an Easter egg–hunt promotion the station sponsored. It was a natural fit: the chicken and eggs. Soon Ted's gigs expanded and multiplied, and he quickly became a crowd pleaser at everything from concerts to movie premieres. What Ted lacked in formal mascot training, he more than made up for with spontaneous antics, incredible comedic timing, and audience connections.

On the Padres' opening night in 1974, KGB sent the chicken to make an appearance in the stands; it also was the first home game that the Padres' new owner, Ray Kroc, attended. The team was playing poorly enough that during the game, Mr. Kroc, relying on his owner prerogative, walked into the public address booth, grabbed the mic from PA announcer John DeMott, and apologized to the fans for the team's lousy performance. I was never sure what drew greater attention, the apology of the owner or the naked man streaking across the outfield and at whom Mr. Kroc was also yelling. The chicken was not star billing that inaugural game night.

As the chicken's popularity grew quickly and dramatically, he was welcomed practically anywhere he went in the community. Being the entrepreneur he was, Ted swiftly parlayed his comedic mime talent to pay raises far exceeding his initial hourly rate of $2. He was being offered paid appearances around the country, and KGB did not approve and would not consent. Ted secured legal help and ultimately gained the right to be known as the Famous Chicken. Despite the presence of the jolly oversized Friar at all home games, I believe fans still think of the Famous Chicken as the official mascot of the Padres.

After his successful legal foray and the design of a new chicken costume, Ted and the Padres formed a pact immediately. The big return to stadium stardom was to be June 29, 1979, when the Padres faced the Houston Astros. The egg was made out of Styrofoam and placed on the plaza concourse under the right-field scoreboard, where everyone could see it during the Padres game leading up to the "Grand Hatching." The plan was to have a California Highway Patrol motorcycle motorcade, with sirens blasting, escort a Loomis armored truck carrying the egg, which would enter from the right-field tunnel and slowly drive around the outfield warning track to gather attention. The egg would be then carefully placed at third base, and the pulsating drumbeat music from the movie *2001: A Space Odyssey* would fill the park.

That night, as more than 47,000 people filed and jostled into the ballpark, the start time was delayed by more than a half hour. Everyone wanted to see the "Grand Hatching." When the crowd was getting restless, the egg was brought in as scripted. It was carefully lowered from the roof of the Loomis truck to the hands of awaiting Padres players, including Eric Rasmussen and Fernando Gonzalez, who placed it at third base. As the egg began to roll around the infield dirt near third base, Ted began kicking from inside the egg to break it open. We had scripted his hatching and assumed it would go as planned, but it went on without a dry run. All I could think of was "don't count your chickens before they hatch." What if he cannot break through the seal? What if he passes out from a lack of air? I am sure it was less than two minutes, but it seemed like an eternity to me. Eventually, out popped the chicken from his Styrofoam shell adorned in his new garb to a standing ovation from the crowd. To this day, Ted confirms it was the loudest and most sustained crowd applause he ever received. After his exaggerated bows to all sections of the stadium, Kurt Bevacqua and John D'Acquisto ran over and hoisted the chicken onto their shoulders.

Well done, chicken.

IT'S CHICKEN TIME. The KGB Chicken was always welcomed, not only to Padres games but also to the office. It wasn't unusual to see the chicken attend a Padres potluck holiday dinner or stop by to give Ray Kroc a gift. (Elten Schiller.)

54

A MAN OF NOTE. Jim Eakle was a Marine pilot who flew helicopters and loved baseball and his Padres. On his own, he brought a tuba to a game to play to rally the fans in the stands. He rooting for the players to score more runs or shut down the opponents. He was the unofficial Padres cheerleader in the 1970s, and after a short while he had free access to San Diego Stadium. Eventually, others joined him, such as Flute Lady and Drum Man. Jim had a easygoing and friendly personality, and as soon as you met him, you wanted to have a beer with him—and more than likely did. (Elten Schiller.)

A BELL RINGER. The Padres Friar, otherwise known as Carol Fitzgerald, carrying a bell, poses for the fans during an early-1970s Camera Day. (Madres.)

LET'S GO PADRES. The Friar and the KGB Chicken could make 2,500 fans sound like 3,000 fans during any Padres game in the mid-1970s. These cheerleaders were not employees of the Padres but rather outgoing, exuberant Padres fans who just happened to be wearing costumes and tirelessly rooting for the Padres. (Jim Eakle.)

55

DON'T EGG HIM ON. On June 29, 1979, the 10-foot Styrofoam egg atop the Loomis armored truck enters San Diego Stadium from the right-field tunnel and begins its California Highway Patrol escort with sirens blasting to third base. (Mike McDuffee.)

THE CHICKEN'S BIG BREAK. Once the egg was lowered onto the third base dirt, the theme music from *2001: A Space Odyssey* started playing, and the chicken started kicking from inside the egg to break it open and reveal his new costume. The crowd around the egg and chicken include members of the media. Astros players couldn't resist and stepped out of their dugout to catch all the action. (Tom Walsh.)

COWBOY. For a number of years in the 1980s, a single person sold the *San Diego Tribune* to fans in the stands. No one knew his name, but everyone called him "Cowboy." He had a ritual of throwing his arms up in the air as if he had just knocked out Sonny Listen or kicked a field goal when he sold his last newspaper at the bottom of the plaza-level seats. The response from the fans, regardless of what was going on the field between the Padres and opponents, was a roar of approval combined with applause. (Jan Brooks.)

WING MAN. The KGB Chicken put on a Santa beard for a Padres front office Christmas party and at one point compared left wings with Padres pitcher Randy Jones, who had just won the 1976 Cy Young Award. Note that the chicken's "barn door" is open. (Author's collection.)

SANTA CHICKEN. If anyone bought $25 or more of merchandise from the Padres' gift shop in mid-December 1983, they got to sit on Santa Chicken's lap and have their picture taken. It was a deal I couldn't pass up, and now I have this treasured photograph as a keepsake. (Ben Valley.)

WHAT A DRAG. In 1978, Ozzie Smith was a rookie shortstop trying to stay up in the big leagues. He is concentrating on making his practice throws to first between innings, while the chicken helps the San Diego Stadium ground crew drag the infield. (Madres.)

BAD IDEA. In 1992, the Padres unveiled Bluepper as their new mascot, attempting to replace the San Diego Chicken. It was the brainchild of Andy Strasberg. Bluepper was not well received—and that is wording it kindly. Needless to say, the fans hated him. They were often heard chanting, "We want the chicken" and derisively nicknamed Bluepper "Down in Front." Bluepper did not return for the 1993 season, thank goodness. (Larry Carpa.)

MY NEIGHBOR. I was too ashamed to tell people that the Padres' mascot Bluepper lived on my block, but he did. Here he is posing with my wife, Jeannette, and her sister Mary Lou Smith on his way to work. (Mike McDuffee.)

CATS AND DOGS. Once the Padres had made a deal with PETCO for the naming rights to their new downtown ballpark, it was only a matter of time before PETCO's mascots would be regulars at Padres games. Here is Red Ruff, a dog, and Blue Mews, a cat, mingling in PETCO's left-field bleachers during a Padres game. (Larry Carpa.)

DOLL FACE. The Swinging Friar made a triumphant return in the late 1990s. He looked friendly and knew his role on and off the field. He became a cheerleader and would be on the field for pre-game activities and in the stands for photo ops. The Padres gift shop started to make available many items that utilized his image, including a plush doll. Once again, the Padres had a mascot they could call their own. (Larry Carpa.)

Seven

MARCH GLADNESS

Back in the 1970s, the Padres held spring training in Yuma, Arizona, about a two- to three-hour drive from San Diego. Driving 120 miles each way made the trip something fans could enjoy in a single March day. A typical fan could get on the road early Sunday morning, have breakfast in Yuma, and then head over to Sun Desert Stadium for an afternoon game.

I had not taken a day off since I began working on January 2, 1975, so I opted to drive over to Yuma so that I could be part of the spring-training scene. Leaving late on a Saturday after work, I arrived near 8:30 p.m. and went to the complex housing the Padres' offices and locker rooms. I immediately looked for Doc Mattei, the club's traveling secretary, and asked if he could help arrange for me a one-night stay at a Yuma hotel. Doc thought I was kidding. First, there were then only a handful of motels in Yuma, and most had been booked months ago for spring training. Doc did provide a solution by assembling a cot in the middle of the Padres' clubhouse, and I was set.

Immediately I flashed back to the 1962 movie *Safe at Home*, starring Mickey Mantle and Roger Maris. In the movie, a kid sneaks into the Yankees' spring training facility and falls asleep in the middle of the clubhouse on a table. I remember how envious I was of that kid at the time, and now 13 years later I was playing the role in real life. My first night at spring training I "had to" sleep in the middle of the locker room on an old Navy cot.

The following spring, the Padres had invited Joe Pepitone to spring training. Joe was the last connection to the Yankees of my childhood, so my wife, Patti, and I decided to drive over and see a Sunday game and brought another couple with us. Before leaving, I called and made arrangements for tickets to the game, and I told a couple of front-office Padres employees that I really wanted to be introduced to Pepitone.

As soon as I arrived, Padres public relations director Mike Ryan saw me and took me into the clubhouse to meet "Pepi." A few minutes later, on one of the auxiliary practice fields, general manager Bob Fontaine introduced me again. And then not long after that, Jerry Coleman introduced us still another time. "OK already, I met this guy a million times," Pepi said after either our fourth or fifth introduction.

The Cubs were the opponent, and the game was tied in the bottom of the ninth inning. With a runner on second, Pepi stepped up to the plate and dug his cleats in the desert dirt batter's box. The count went to 2-1 when Pepi lined a hanging slider to right-center field and the runner on second scored to win the game.

In a very unprofessional manner, I exploded with a cheer and left my seat and ran onto the field to congratulate Joe as if it was a game-winning hit in a World Series game. I was patting Joe on the back as he made his way to the Padres' locker room while my wife and friends were staring in silent amazement at me. As Joe began the walk down the left-field line, I was right alongside him, sidestep-walking and repeating what a great game he played, how he got the game-winning hit, and that he would one day be a part of this great Padres team. When we got into the locker room,

I was still there, and while Joe was undressing he finally said, "Are you going to take a shower with me, too?" That snapped me back to reality, and I meekly responded, "No, I'll wait here."

Joe walked off, towels around his waist and over his shoulder while I stood there almost frozen. When he returned, as he was getting dressed, I was at a loss for what to do when I heard him say, "Hey, you wanna get some pizza?" I am positive I replied with one of those tough-guy movie lines, "Are youse kiddin' me?"

I said "yes" as Joe explained he was meeting up with Rudy Meoli and Carmen Fanzone at Bronx Pizza not far from the Padres' spring-training site. We walked out of the clubhouse and there were Patti and the couple we had driven over with from San Diego. Patti wanted to know what was going on, and I explained that Joe and I and a couple of the guys were going to get pizza. I told her to meet us there. At the restaurant, we ordered pizzas and pitchers of beer, and I positioned myself right next to Joe. The tables were the kind that have only four chairs and are bolted into the floor and do not move. Joe, Carmen, Rudy, and I were at our table, while Patti and our friends sat at another one nearby. Patti's looks were laser-like, but I was not moving. And, you know something? Pizza never tasted so good.

HAIR TODAY. Joe Pepitone was an invitee to the Padres' spring training in 1976. His major-league career was winding down, but he was still famous for being the first baseball player to use a hair dryer in a clubhouse. He didn't make the team out of spring training and played for the Padres Triple-A team, the Hawaii Islanders. Pepi only got into 13 games that season for the Islanders and never returned to the big leagues. (Roger Morse.)

A Team of Steal. The Padres' 1980 spring-training dugout is pictured just moments before a game. On the top step are Ozzie Smith and Gene Richards. This was a special year for the franchise, because Jerry Coleman traded in the broadcast booth for the dugout and was the team manager. One of the benchmarks of the team was that Jerry liked the running game, so there were three Padres players who stole over 50 bases: Smith (57), Richards (61), and Jerry Mumphrey (52). (Madres.)

Goose Legs. One of the reasons the Padres won the National League pennant in 1984 was Rich "Goose" Gossage. He anchored the bullpen and was so intense on the mound that it could be felt in the stands. Gossage had a 10-6 record, all in relief, in 1984. The anticipation of the Padres was building in March 1985, when I shot this during spring training in Yuma, Arizona. My daughter Blake Tucker is looking up at Goose Gossage and is about to ask him to sign her program. (Terry Tucker.)

PADRES' GOLD. Bobby Tolan looks over at the photographer on his way to the dugout. One of the challenges of spring training in Yuma was what the players refer to as a "high sky," which means when a baseball is hit in the air, it is difficult to judge because of the blue-sky background. For some reason, the Yuma sky was different than San Diego's blue skies. (Madres.)

TAKE A LAP. Benito Santiago is getting his running in on the outfield warning track. One of my favorite memories is Benny's ability to throw runners out at any base from his knees and not take a wind up or a step. I haven't seen another catcher do that since. (Duane Arnold.)

GOING HOME BABY.
Jim Davenport's playing career was exclusively with the San Francisco Giants as their third baseman from 1958 to 1970. Jim was the Padres' third-base coach in 1974 and 1975, and fans would see him moving around the Yuma complex carrying bags of baseballs from one field to another or hitting grounders to infielders. During Padres games, Jim would get the manager's sign and relay it to the batter. As the third-base coach, it was his judgment if a player should try to make it home after rounding third. (Madres.)

LITTLE JOEY. Joey Cora played for the Padres in 1989 and 1990. He attended Vanderbilt University and showed great hustle when he arrived on the San Diego scene. But, his impact on baseball blossomed after he left the Padres and played for other organizations the following nine years. Joey's time with the Mariners actually was highlighted and best remembered when he broke down and cried in the dugout sitting on the bench when the Mariners were eliminated from the playoffs in 1995. The image is heartwarming and quickly endeared him to Mariner baseball fans. After his playing career, Joey was a coach for Ozzie Guillen for the Marlins. He has a desire to be a big-league manager and had a taste of what it was like when he was the interim Miami Marlin manager after Ozzie was suspended for five games in 2012 due to his comments about Fidel Castro. (Larry Carpa.)

UP CLOSE. Doug McWilliams, the official Topps baseball card photographer, would shoot four to five different poses of every player if he was cooperative, and many times only one of the shots would be used on a card. A couple of years ago, McWilliams generously donated all the slides he took at spring training throughout his career to the National Baseball Hall of Fame in Cooperstown. Here, Bobby Tolan is kneeling for his close up. (Author's collection.)

ROGER RAMJET. One of the responsibilities of Padres players is to sign team baseballs before every game. The baseballs, once signed by the entire team, would then be used by the front office in a variety of ways, such as gifts, charity auction donations, and so forth. Dick Sharon had a unique sense of humor, because instead of signing his name, he signed a cartoon character's name, Roger Ramjet, thus ruining every baseball that his teammates had spent the time autographing. Dick must have needed a good lawyer, because here he is talking with a prominent and widely respected San Diego attorney and Padres fan Frank Howard in Yuma. (Madres.)

A TOWERING DRIVE. The most recognizable landmark in Yuma, Arizona, is the water tower, located behind third base of the Padres' spring-training complex. The tower can be seen for miles, as the landscape is flat. It is now decorated for special holidays and has become the pride of Yuma. (Duane Arnold.)

COUNTRY HARDBALL. Garth Brooks loved baseball so much that for a period of time he would participate in spring training with the Padres. Garth quickly realized that getting a hit was a lot more difficult on a baseball field in Peoria, Arizona, then in a Nashville recording studio. He is seen here in March 1998. (Larry Carpa.)

ART WORKS. Gene Locklear is an artist of great renown. He also had a sense of humor, because every now and then when he played for the Padres he would sometimes find a feather and place it sticking out of his baseball cap. His teammates called him "Chief." In 1994, the baseball card company Upper Deck featured his artwork of baseball legends on baseball cards. He is proud of his American Indian heritage and has paintings of sport greats, not only from baseball but football and golf as well. In addition to sports themes, his specialties include Western-themed paintings. He is still a resident of San Diego and has painting exhibits around the country. (Madres.)

A CUBBIE. There are a number of baseball players who in the minds of fans are always associated with one organization even though they ended their careers with another team. Glenn Beckert is best remembered as the second baseman for the Chicago Cubs, but he played for the Padres in 1974 and 1975. When Beckert did announce his retirement from baseball, Padres broadcaster Jerry Coleman said, "I hope before Glenn goes, he'll come up here so we can give him a big hug and kiss, because that's the kind of guy he is." (Madres.)

YOU DON'T KNOW JACK. After Jack Murphy passed away in 1980, San Diego Stadium was renamed Jack Murphy Stadium. It was a tribute to the *San Diego Union* sportswriter who campaigned for a multipurpose stadium in San Diego with the hope that it would attract a major-league baseball team. Many San Diegans have no idea who he was or what he looked like. Here's Jack turning towards the photographer at Padres spring training in 1976. Jack's brother Bob Murphy was the New York Mets' beloved broadcaster for many years. (Madres.)

PROMISES, PROMISES. In 1987, I took my son David Magnuson to spring training in Yuma, Arizona. David was a fan of Benito Santiago, and before a game he asked if he could have his photograph taken with the catcher. Benito promised he would after the game. The Padres lost, and as the players walked dejectedly across the road to the locker room, David reminded me of Benito's promise. I assured him the team was not in a fan-friendly mood. He agreed, and we walked with the crowd toward the parking lot. As we did, Benito stopped, looked around, saw us in the crowd, and stopped pedestrian traffic to pose for the picture he promised my six-year-old son. The photograph still hangs in my living room. I have continued to respect Benito and how he put a child's wish above his own feelings. Benny has never done anything to let my son's or my view of him become clouded—a true role model. (Kathy Lankin.)

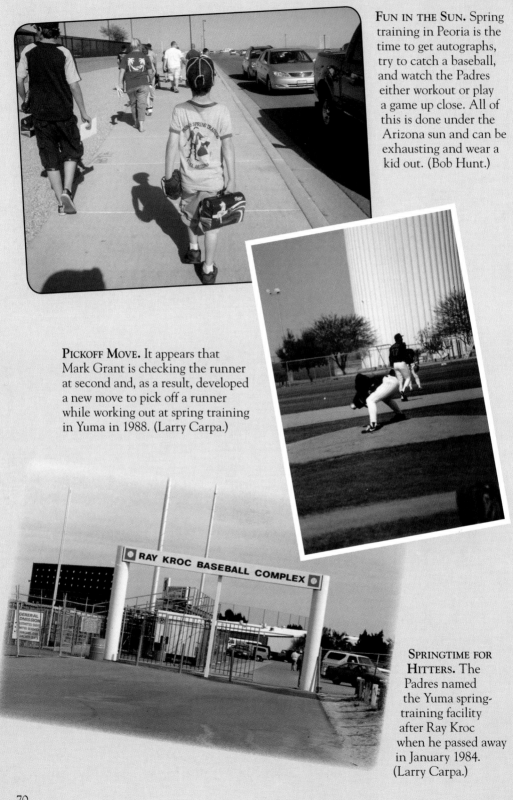

Fun in the Sun. Spring training in Peoria is the time to get autographs, try to catch a baseball, and watch the Padres either workout or play a game up close. All of this is done under the Arizona sun and can be exhausting and wear a kid out. (Bob Hunt.)

Pickoff Move. It appears that Mark Grant is checking the runner at second and, as a result, developed a new move to pick off a runner while working out at spring training in Yuma in 1988. (Larry Carpa.)

Springtime for Hitters. The Padres named the Yuma spring-training facility after Ray Kroc when he passed away in January 1984. (Larry Carpa.)

MARCHING TO PEORIA. The Padres spring-training site left Yuma, Arizona, in 1993 so the team could be closer to the other major-league teams training in the Phoenix area. It shares the Peoria facility with the Seattle Mariners, and it has become a spring destination for fans from around the country. (Madres.)

PADRES MADRES. The Madres are in their seats to catch a Padres game against the Angels in Palm Springs in 1984. They are decked out in Padres brown and yellow caps and shirts, and one Madres is proudly wearing her "I'm a Madre" button on her cap. This fan group is still in existence and provides funds for youth baseball teams around San Diego County. Its dedication and enthusiasm is unparalleled in major-league baseball. (Madres.)

STREEETCH. Willie McCovey was in Padres spring-training camp in 1975 getting ready for the upcoming season. Willie had a few nicknames, and because of his height (6 feet, 4 inches), one of them was "Stretch." Here's Stretch stretching. Willie hit a total of 52 homers while with the Padres in three seasons. (Cathy Carey.)

PADRES QB FAN. Chargers quarterback and Football Hall of Famer Dan Fouts was best friends with Padres coach Whitey Wietelmann. Fouts would often come to Yuma to watch the Padres play and spend some time with his buddy. Seated between them is Bruce Wick. (Larry Carpa.)

WHERE ART THOU ROMO? The Padres realized that one of the attractions for baseball fans from Mexico would be to have one of their countrymen on the team. Right-hander Vincente Romo was born in Baja California and started his major-league career pitching for the Dodgers in 1968. Romo then pitched for three other major-league teams before he caught on with the Padres in 1973. After two years with San Diego and a record of 7-8, Romo returned to Mexico to play professional baseball in his homeland. (Madres.)

SMILE. Not every photograph taken by Topps photographer Doug McWilliams becomes a baseball card. Here's Tito Fuentes kneeling for his close-up wearing a sweatband that reads "TITO" on the outside of his cap. Fortunately, that fashion statement didn't catch on with anyone else. Prior to joining the Padres, Tito Fuentes played for the Giants and after a near beaning was quoted as saying, "They shouldn't throw at me. I'm the father of five or six kids." (Author's collection.)

Eight

YARD WORK

No doubt every major-league club has a fan or booster organization. The Padres are no different. Organized more than 40 years ago, the Madres remain a vital and enthusiastic group of women who love and promote their Padres like no others.

The Madres were originally founded in 1972 by player wives and Joy Harvey, wife of former National League umpire and Baseball Hall of Famer Doug Harvey. Consistent with the changing times, the organization, while remaining predominantly made up of female members, has opened membership to males as well. The San Diego Madres is a nonprofit organization whose mission is provide all children in San Diego County the opportunity to play baseball and softball through financial support of dozens of leagues.

When I joined the Padres in 1975, the love affair with the Madres was instantaneous. The support the organization provided me in fulfilling my job was both generous and dependable. On many occasions when I was confronted with a thorny situation, the Madres stepped up and provided countless hours of free labor. They helped all projects they were involved with succeed, whether it was helping distribute Junior Padres tickets; addressing, stuffing, and mailing thousands of envelopes; or even punching All-Star ballots for Padres nominees. One of the many times the Madres came to my rescue was when the Padres hosted the 1978 All-Star Game. One of my responsibilities for that event was to arrange for each visiting media member or club representative to receive a complimentary gift bag of items. The 1977 All-Star Game gift bag contained nine souvenir items, and I felt San Diego needed to make a better effort and impress all the recipients. I set out to secure more souvenir donations and shatter the total of nine items. I asked many local and national businesses, and to my surprise we ended up with 46 quality items that would be included in each of the goody bags. My challenge was suddenly to coordinate filling the bags.

Because items kept coming in, it was only a week before the game when I reached out to the Madres to see if they could help. They suggested an assembly line to get the job done. Spread out over several tables in the stadium parking lot, more than two dozen Madres picked up an item at a time and packed the bags. My desire to supervise and help was shunned, and I was told by the Madres to go find something else to do because "we have it handled." And, they did—perfectly. By the time the Padres again hosted the All-Star Game in 1992, the goody-bag tradition had ended. Undaunted, and remembering what the Madres and I had jointly accomplished, I pleaded with and somehow convinced Major League Baseball officials to allow us to bring back the bag. It was a huge success again.

The unselfish and generous efforts of the Madres have provided financial support to over 500 youth teams during the past four decades and countless thousands of hours volunteering in a multitude of ways. Throughout the years, the Madres have maintained a documentation history of their participation as Padres supporters, compiling dozens of scrapbooks and, perhaps most importantly from my perspective, thousands of photographs documenting all the organization has done. The snapshot and photo collection of the Madres is fascinating and comprehensive.

The core of the Madres' activities is probably their multiple group lunches each year with Padres coaches, players, announcers, and front-office executives as their special guests.

Throughout this book, you will see some of those Madres photographs, and by their request, none of the photo credits are given to individuals but rather to the organization. Suffice it to say that the photographs were taken by many dedicated Madres members. There were many people and groups who extended helping hands to me during my Padres career, and tops among them are the Madres. Incorporating their Padres snapshots, they have once again lent a helping hand.

I urge you to consider becoming a part of one of San Diego's richest baseball traditions, the San Diego Madres (www.sandiegomadres.org).

GAME OVER. The 1984 Padres beat the Chicago Cubs and were headed to the World Series to face the Detroit Tigers. The one-hopper to Graig Nettles, who threw to Alan Wiggins at second, started a celebration that lasted for a couple of days. This is the mob scene comprised mostly of Padres players, coaches, and media to start the celebration. (Tom Larwin.)

NL NIGHTMARE. The annual All-Star Game came back to San Diego in 1992 and was played on the same field as in 1978. The dream game quickly became a nightmare. Before the National League could come to bat in the bottom of the first inning, the score was 4-0. It got worse. The final score was 13-6 for the American League. If you take a close look at who played in the game, you will find that 16 former, current, or future Padres participated in the Midsummer Classic that night. (Tom Larwin.)

T&T. I took this photograph of Ted Williams and Tony Gwynn and thought how remarkable it is that two of baseball's greatest hitters played for the Padres: Ted was on the Pacific Coast League Padres when he graduated from high school in 1936, and Tony played his entire major-league career for the Padres, beginning in 1982 and ending after the 2001 season. (Jay Maxwell.)

No Fraternizing. Rule 3.09 states: "Players on opposing teams shall not fraternize at any time while in uniform." In this 1978 snapshot, you can see Padres players Dave Winfield (far right), Oscar Gamble, Derrel Thomas, and Broderick Perkins visiting with Dodgers Steve Garvey, Ron Cey, Dusty Baker, Rick Monday, Davey Lopes, and Lee Lacy in the outfield of San Diego Stadium before a game. Where are the baseball police when you need them? (Tom Larwin.)

Red, White, and Blue. The 2013 Padres home opener started with a large American flag unfurled on the field at PETCO Park. Most of the photographs taken that day are taken from the stands facing towards the outfield. This was taken from the building past right field and gives a unique point of view of the pre-game ceremony. The Padres beat the Dodgers 9-3. (Darius Aram.)

POST GAME. You can tell that the game is over by the number of empty cups scattered around the Padres' dugout. You can also tell that the Padres won—otherwise a Padres player would not be interviewed. More than likely, Bip Roberts either won it for the Padres or played a significant role in the win. (Larry Carpa.)

AREN'T YOU ARCHI? Archi Cianfrocco played for the Padres from 1993 to 1998. His Padres fan clubs included Archi's Army and the CianfrocCrew. Archi won the Cooperstown Baseball Hall of Fame Weekend Home Run Derby on August 4, 1997. A dubious distinction is that Archi was the batter for the Padres on May 9, 1994, when Cincinnati Reds left-hander Tom Browning broke his arm throwing a pitch in the sixth inning. Browning sustained a fracture about three inches below the shoulder, where the deltoid tendon connects the bone to the shoulder muscles. (Larry Carpa.)

PADRES BACKERS. The San Diego Ted Williams Chapter of the Society for American Baseball Research (SABR) spent a day in 2005 taking photographs of interesting people and happenings at PETCO Park. (Ron Andreassi.)

NICE CATCH. Playing the outfield during the 1992 All-Star Game Home Run Derby is Padres employee Cheryl Smith, who had played softball for Arizona State just a few years earlier. Once the fans realized it wasn't a guy snagging those wicked line drives, their attention was focused on the slick-fielding, fundamentally sound outfielder. (Larry Carpa.)

THE STARE. Phil Clark gives a stare as this photograph is taken while he and Andy Ashby are signing autographs at Qualcomm. Phil and his brother Jerald both hold the distinction of playing for the Padres and also in the Nippon Professional Baseball League. In 1997, Phil, while playing in the Japanese league, trailed only Ichiro Suzuki in batting average. (Madres.)

DEEP-KNEE TALK. Dennis Martinez of the Montreal Expos, who was known as "El Presidente," squats down to have a conversation with Padres pitcher Eric Show. Although Show holds the record for most wins (100) by a Padres pitcher, his notoriety comes from two things: he revealed in 1984 that he was a member of the John Birch Society, and he threw the pitch to Pete Rose that broke Ty Cobb's all-time career hit record of 4,192 on September 11, 1985, in Cincinnati. After giving up the record hit, he sat down on the mound while the celebration took place. Show died prematurely from a drug overdose in 1994. (Larry Carpa.)

PROOF POSITIVE. San Diego went crazy in 1984 when the Padres beat the Cubs and won the National League pennant. This is photographic proof that my brother Mitch was at the firs- ever Padres World Series game in 1984. Unfortunately, the Padres lost to the Tigers in the Fall Classic and won only one game. (Gary Holdinghausen.)

DOWN MEMORY LANE FIELD. This was the right-field fence at the San Diego Padres Pacific Coast League home, Lane Field, in the 1940s. You can see the top of the Sante Fe Depot beyond the fence. Local baseball fans love to tell stories about how far home runs hit over this fence traveled, explaining that some would bounce onto a freight car headed to points north and thereby traveled over 200 miles. (Duane Dimock.)

RICKEY TALKS ABOUT RICKEY. Rickey Henderson leads all major-league players who have talked about themselves in the third person. He played for the Padres in 1996–1997 and 2001. One of the best Ricky stories that he tells is about when he played for the Oakland Athletics. They sent Ricky a $1 million check, which he framed and prominently placed on his wall instead of cashing it, because as a kid he always dreamed of having $1 million. Eventually, when the A's realized that the check had not cleared, they contacted Ricky, only to discover the check had become a keepsake hanging in his den. (Penny Altman.)

IN A MOMENT. On July 19, 1982, just before Tony Gwynn got up to bat for the first time in the major leagues, I snuck down near the dugout and shot this photograph. Seated closest to me are, from front to back, Garry Templeton, Dick Williams, Terry Kennedy, Tony Gwynn, and Tim Lollar, and farther down is the Padres trainer, Dick Dent. It is moments before Gwynn would go to bat. I couldn't believe that the Padres had drafted a basketball player from San Diego State. Little did I or anyone else realize that Gwynn would go to bat 10,232 times and hit his way into the Baseball Hall of Fame with a lifetime batting average of .338. (Fred O. Rodgers.)

CLOSE UP AND PERSONAL. Here is a unique angle of the Padres' low third-base cameraman working at covering the game on September 5, 2004. (Ron Andreassi.)

CENTER DEEP AND STEEP. In 1969, when the Padres started to play at San Diego Stadium, until 1972, it was 420 feet to center field, 375 feet in the power alleys, and 330 feet down the line. And, that's not all: the fence was 18 feet high. In 1970 and 1972, Padres first baseman Nate Colbert hit 38 homers. Did I mention it was 420 feet to center field? (Bob W. Taylor.)

BIG MAC SUNDAY. Willie McCovey made his major-league debut on July 30, 1959, and played for the San Francisco Giants. Willie went 4-4 against future Hall of Famer Robin Roberts, with two triples and two singles. Willie played for the Padres (1974–1976) during his Hall of Fame career. He tied Ted Williams, Rickey Henderson, and Omar Vizquel for homering in four decades and is one of only 29 players to have played major-league baseball in four decades. His vicious line drive that ended the Giants' bid to become world champs in the 1962 World Series became immortalized in a *Peanuts* cartoon on December 22, 1962. The cartoon depicts Charlie Brown and Linus brooding silently for three panels, and then Charlie Brown screams, "Why couldn't McCovey have hit the ball just three feet higher?" The next month, on January 28, 1963, the same two *Peanuts* characters are once again sitting in similar positions for three panels, and in the fourth panel Charlie Brown screams, "Why couldn't McCovey have hit the ball just two feet higher?" Coincidentally, McCovey, who was known as "Big Mac" and played for the Padres when the team was owned by Ray Kroc, the owner of McDonald's, served Big Macs. The Padres staged a promotion during every Sunday home game in 1975; when the Padres won, the ticket stub from that game could be exchanged for a Big Mac at any of 23 San Diego McDonald's. (Madres.)

Tony Had the Will to Win. The 1989 National League batting race came down to the last game of the season. The Padres' Tony Gwynn was battling the Giants' Will Clark for the title, and the teams played each other on the last day of the season at San Diego Stadium. The race was so close that every at-bat for Will and Tony would change who the leader was by a decimal point. On October 1, 1989, a thoughtful fan kept the crowd informed as Tony Gwynn won the title. (Jan Brooks.)

Jump Start. To get the Padres jump-started during the 1984 post-season, shortstop Garry Templeton took off his cap and quickly waved it around to get fans excited about being in the 1984 playoffs. It worked, as the Padres came back to beat the Cubs in the best-of-five series. (Madres.)

FUHGEDDABOUTIT. The remedy for blowing a save for a reliever is to forget it, but it is not always easy to do. Players are human and sensitive, and they feel that they let the team down after losing a game. Trevor Hoffman had 601 saves and 40 blown saves. Here's Trevor sitting in the Padres dugout, thinking through what has just gone wrong on the field. In a short amount of time, Trevor would get up, go into the clubhouse, face the media, and answer all their questions before going home. The next day, yesterday's blown save would be a distant memory. (Larry Carpa.)

FINS WINS. Steve Finley provided many dramatic endings to Padres games, either with his bat or glove, while a member of the team from 1995 to 1998. (Larry Carpa.)

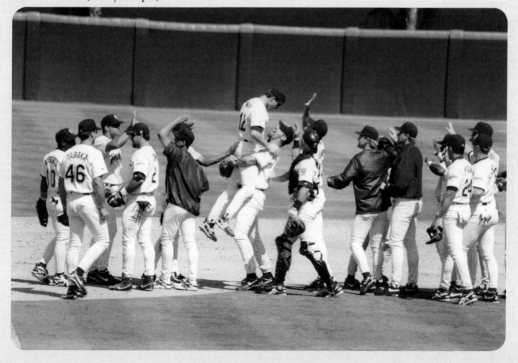

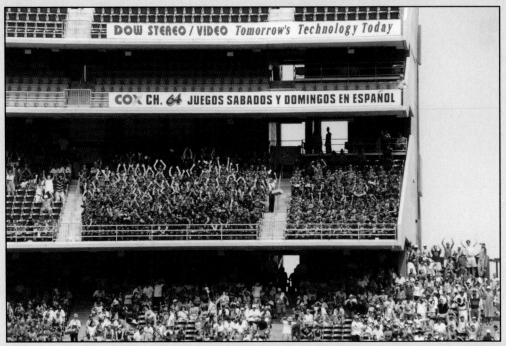

OORAH. One of the traditions that the Padres have had at their Sunday games over the years is hosting the Marines and/or Navy recruits. Watching them march in and leave is exciting and very patriotic. In this 1988 photograph, Marines are participating in the wave at San Diego Stadium. The highlight of the afternoon is when the official song of the Marines or Navy is played and the recruits stand at attention. It all ends with a thunderous round of applause from appreciative fans. (Larry Carpa.)

NAME GAME. Gene Tenace was the Padres' catcher from 1977 to 1980. His first name is Fury, and he was born Fiore Gino Tennaci. His nickname is "Steamboat," which was given to him by his grandfather on his mother's side, who said that as a kid Gene walked like a clumsy big steamboat; his close friends shortened it and just called him "Boat." (Madres.)

Nine

BONUS BABIES

This chapter of photographs has no relevance to the fact that from 1947 through 1965, an amateur baseball player who signed a contract for a specified amount of money was called a "bonus baby" and was required to be on the 25-man roster for a full season. These snapshots could not be categorized in any of the other chapters, and since they were deemed something good and more than expected or required, such as the 1978 All-Star Game, they are placed here.

Whether "Tinker to Evers to Chance" or Schiller to Wietelmann to tradition, the Padres were hosts for the 1978 All-Star Game, and believe it or not the midsummer contest in San Diego gave rise to several traditions.

Padres vice president of business Elten Schiller had asked me to take a swing at designing the game ticket, and I simply put the Swinging Friar inside a large star with the other team logos floating around it. I also volunteered that I thought a uniform patch of the All-Star Game Friar with a star background worn on the sleeve would help promote the game.

Elten had attended the All-Star Game in Yankee Stadium the previous year and also the teams' workouts on Monday before the game. He told me that when he stepped off the Major League Baseball charter bus he thought of me and how I had shared with him all the times I stood outside Yankee Stadium in hopes of seeing one of the baseball greats enter the ballpark. He noted that there were dozens of young kids hanging out near the entrances also hoping for a glimpse of one of the stars. Elten shared with me that inside the stadium for the workout it was empty except for the players, coaches, press, and a few officials from the two leagues, all of whom were down at field level. The seats were empty, as fans were not permitted to watch the practice.

Remembering his experience, when it came time for the game in San Diego Elten would not miss an opportunity to promote the sport and accommodate the fans. He decided to open the San Diego Stadium gates for the workout day preceding the game. Admission and parking were free, and Coca-Cola volunteered to be the sponsor of the event. Fans who could not afford or secure tickets would still get a chance to see the world's best up close.

Those who came for the workout were treated to a show unlike any before, and as a result that became one of the featured events in future years.

One of the Padres coaches, Whitey Wietelmann, had about six dozen of the highly compressed "rabbit baseballs" remaining from our Old Timer's Day. I had them specially made for that game to ensure that when an old-timer hit the ball it had a better chance of reaching the seats. Without a word, Whitey made sure the National League hitters were served up the special balls during their batting practice. As the American Leaguers looked on in bewildered amazement, one National League hitter after another crushed pitches deep into the stands. When it was the American League's turn in the batting cage, the regular balls were used, and many landed in the deep outfield, with only a few hitting the seats. Whitey revealed his secret much later with a twinkling grin.

From that little baseball adjustment by Whitey and free fan event via Elten grew the long-ball hitting contests and fan workout days that are now an integral part of the annual All-Star Game festivities.

TAKE A POSITION. Darrel Thomas was cool on and off the baseball field. During his 15-year career, Darrel played every position except pitcher. He was primarily a second baseman but also played the outfield, even catching six games in his career. He was with the Padres from 1972 until 1974 and then again in 1978. Here he is walking through the stands at San Diego Stadium wearing shades and a sleeveless vest that probably came from Bill Gamble's men's shop. (Madres.)

SOCK IT TO ME. Max West grew up in Southern California and made his big-league debut in 1938. He played outfield and first base for the Padres in 1947, 1949, and 1950. He went to high school with my mom, and they remained good friends all these years. My mom had this great picture of Max with one foot on his car. I don't know what the circumstances were, but this is a treasured family heirloom. After his playing career ended, he owned a sporting-goods store in Alhambra, California. West died of brain cancer at age 87 in 2003. (Phil Galvin.)

GOOD VIBRATIONS. Prior to a Beach Boys concert after a Padres game, from left to right, Mike Love, Andy Strasberg, and Bruce Johnston start warming up their vocal chords. Fortunately, Strasberg didn't sing on stage. (JC Crouch.)

HE PARKED IT! Because of the enormous size of the parking lot that surrounded San Diego Stadium, tailgating became part of the Padres baseball experience. Fans would barbecue, drink, play catch, and party before and after the game. Some fans drove around in their "ready to party" or tailgate vehicles all year. (Jim Eakle.)

89

FOR THE BIRDS. In 2013, I was sitting in PETCO's upper deck minding my own business and enjoying an August ball game while the Cubs were in town. Suddenly, a seagull flew in and started looking around the empty seats like he was trying to remember where he was sitting during last night's game. He stayed for two innings, then gave up and flew away. (Leslie Hanson.)

CHALK TALK. The Padres were on the road for a quick trip and a three-game series in Atlanta during the 1982 season. Our group was given a very special "behind the scenes" tour of the Padres clubhouse at San Diego Stadium as a "thank you" for all the volunteer hours we did for the Padres front office that year. We were thrilled to be in the Padres' locker room, and everyone was fascinated with the travel instructions for the players on the chalkboard. Unfortunately, the Padres won only one of the three games against the Braves on that road trip. (Madres.)

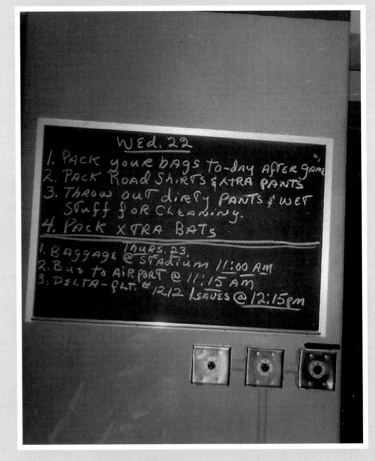

FOR THE AGES. The Padres staged an incredible old-timers game in August 1972, bringing back former major-league and minor-league stars of the past. Among the invited guests was Casey Stengel, who wore a uniform that depicted every name of the seven major-league teams he had an association with as a player or manager. Interesting to note is that Casey was at one point in his illustrious career associated with each New York team: the Dodgers, Giants, Yankees, and Mets. Padres coach Dave Garcia, a longtime resident of San Diego and considered to be one of the nicest, smartest, and most dedicated baseball men the game has known, went over to pay his respects to the "Old Professor" before the game got underway. (Elten Schiller.)

I DO, I DO. The Padres traveling secretary John Mattei was the first employee hired when the Padres became a major-league team. He was known as "Doc" because he was a podiatrist. In the late 1970s, Doc got married at San Diego Stadium's home plate in between games of a double header when the Dodgers were in town to play the Padres. The bride and groom march down the aisle (first-base line) with players holding bats to form an archway. (Val Schiller.)

SPEAKING OF UMPS. Former American League umpire Ed Runge was part of the Padres' speaker's bureau in the 1970s and 1980s. He had some great baseball stories and always made our group laugh. He always used the same opening line after being introduced, "That's the most applause I ever received since I was hit with a beer bottle in Cleveland working third base when the Red Sox were in town to play the Indians." (Madres.)

ELEPHANT ON THIRD BASE. The punch line to one of the dozens of elephant jokes is "walk the elephant and pitch to the giraffe." It's probably not practical if the elephant is leading off the inning, because as all baseball fans know, walking the first batter to start an inning usually means trouble. To make my case, here's a picture I took when I was kid attending the circus performance held at Westgate Park, home of the PCL Padres, in 1963. As you can plainly see, the elephant is on third base and can score now on a hit, sacrifice fly, wild pitch, or passed ball. (William Plante.)

BOW TIE. Terry Kennedy wears an oversized bow tie and cap for a television commercial shoot promoting Camera Day in the mid-1980s. (Ron Seaver.)

A BANNER YEAR. Tony Gwynn's accomplishment of reaching the 3,000-hit mark was celebrated with a special banner hanging from the light ring at Jack Murphy Stadium in 1999. (Mike Ortman.)

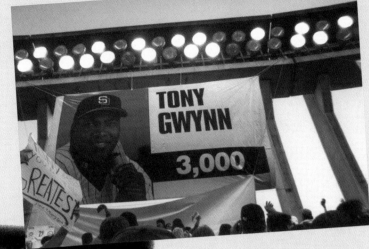

UNIFORMLY 9. During a Padres old-timers' game in 1972, these three sluggers got together and started talking baseball. From left to right are Yankee great Joe DiMaggio, PCL Padres slugger Luke Easter (who also played for the Cleveland Indians), and the Padres' Nate Colbert, who, after 40 years, is still the team's all-time home run leader with 163. It is curious to note that each player at one point in his career wore no. 9 (DiMaggio with the Yankees, Easter with the Indians, and Colbert with the Tigers). (Elten Schiller.)

THREE 19. Tony Gwynn walks with his kids, Anthony and Anisha, on a Padres family-day game. In front of the Gwynns is Bruce Bochy. (Larry Carpa.)

AMBOY DUKE. Padres general manager Jack McKeon spent 10 years in the minor leagues and hit .210. Jack would play softball in the mid-1980s with the Padres' front-office team during the winter and was brilliant with the bat. He could hit the ball virtually anywhere he wanted. Naturally, he tried to trade two of our softball players during a game. (J.C. Crouch.)

SNOW JOB. The Colorado Rockies were heading to San Diego for their first time playing the Padres during their inaugural season of 1993. My intention was to create a never-before environment for those fans attending the game at Jack Murphy Stadium. Somehow, some way, we wanted to create the snow-capped Rocky Mountains in the right-field bleachers for the four games in May that season. We teamed up with popular San Diego radio personalities Jeff and Jer and manufactured 25 tons of snow. Most of it went into the seating area, but we also had some in the parking lot so Jeff and Jer could promote it. That's Jeff sitting on top of the man-made snow. The Padres beat the Rockies 4-0, and we drew 15,251 fans the first night. The biggest crowd showed up for the third game, an afternoon game, and over 22,000 fans stopped by to watch the Padres beat Colorado by a score of 5-4 in 11 innings. (Author's collection.)

WISHES CAN COME TRUE. The Padres returned from Chicago after losing the first two games to the Cubs in the 1984 NLCS. It was a best-of-five-game series, so the Padres were one game from elimination. Padres owner Joan Kroc threw out the ceremonial first pitch to the delight of Padres fans on October 4, 1984. The Padres beat the Cubs 11-5 and went on to win the 1984 NL pennant. (J.C. Crouch.)

FULL OF BEANS. The Padres held an old-timers reunion game on August 18, 1972. Dressed in his Padres gold uniform is Dave Roberts, who is listening intently to legendary retired National League umpire Beans Reardon. (Elten Schiller.)

WEDDING BLISS. When this couple's picture showed up on the Padres video board during a late August game in 2013, I found where they were seated and just had to do the Fantography still-photo version. (Author's collection.)

95

BABY STEPS. Karl Wallenda walked the tightrope after the Padres played the Expos on August 31, 1975. The tightrope was 130 feet off the ground, and Padres ushers (with no previous experience or training) had the responsibility of anchoring it underneath. For that one game, there had to be a new ground rule because the wire was now part of the playing field. A ball hitting the wire was in play regardless if it was fair or foul. Thankfully, no baseballs hit the wire during the game, however. (Cathy Carey.)

ONE OF 600. Karl Wallenda begins his tightrope walk across San Diego Stadium. His sister, who at the time lived in La Jolla, was present and, for whatever reason, counted the number of steps (600) it took Wallenda to get from one end to the other. (Cathy Carey.)

RAINOUT. San Diego Padres players, including Jake Peavy, peer at the proverbial ominous clouds looming over the Hall of Fame Game, scheduled to be played in Cooperstown on June 16, 2008. The game against the Chicago Cubs was indeed rained out, and the tradition of two major-league teams playing an exhibition game in Cooperstown on Doubleday Field ended. (Charlie Vascellaro.)

FIELD INSPECTION. A Marine drill instructor takes a break and watches the Padres during batting practice at PETCO Park. (Tom Larwin.)

Ah-Ten–Shun. US Marine recruits get a break and are the guests of the Padres for a Sunday afternoon ball game at PETCO Park. (Kathy Larwin.)

By Design. In 1968, Jerry Dior created the iconic baseball player silhouette that is the MLB logo, adopted by dozens of other sports and businesses. Jerry visited my friend in San Diego in the summer of 2013 and struck a batting stance pose. I took that photograph and filled in the background to match the colors of his famous logo and thereby created his design in his own image. (Sean Kinyon.)

GIVING THANKS. Don Larsen (left) graduated from Point Loma High School and, while pitching for the New York Yankees, tossed a perfect game on October 8, 1956, in Game Five of the World Series. The umpire who had the right-field foul line for that game was another San Diego resident: American League umpire Ed Runge. October 8, 1956, also happened to be Thanksgiving Day in Canada. (Ed Runge.)

NO PARK AT THE PARK. The lamppost warns drivers that they shouldn't park their cars here. In front of 33,272 fans on a gorgeous, partly sunny San Diego Sunday, the local Ted Williams Chapter of the Society for American Baseball Research worked on a project where members brought their camera and took snapshots of what went on at the Padres game at PETCO Park. The date was September 5, 2004, and the only guideline for the amateur photographers was that the focus of the images could not be of the ball game's on-field action. Many members participated, and as a result the chapter collected a unique photo documentation of the day. Unfortunately, the Colorado Rockies beat the Padres 5-2, highlighted by Matt Holliday, Jeromy Burnitz, and Vinny Castilla each hitting a home run. The project was embraced by a number of other SABR chapters around the country and repeated at various major-league ballparks. (Fred O. Rodgers.)

HUT ONE, TWO, THREE. Marine recruits who attended a Sunday Padres game at PETCO Park march out of the stadium after it ended. (Fred O. Rodgers.)

BASEBALL BOUND. I have been a Padres season-ticket holder since 1972. That's my good friend Pete Nunez with my five-month-old son Gary Frank on his lap during a Padres game. Gary attended every Padres opening day with me for 20 consecutive years, starting before he was one year old. It must have worked, because Gary played two seasons of independent minor-league baseball and is now the head varsity baseball coach at La Jolla High School. (Howard Frank.)

HI HO SILVER. The Silver Bullets existed from 1994 to 1997 and was an all-women's baseball team. They would barnstorm, playing 195 games against men's teams during their four-year existence. The concept was the brainchild of former Atlanta Braves front-office executive Bob Hope. The sponsor of the team was Coors Light beer, hence the name of the team. They didn't have a winning season until 1997, when they had a record of 23-22. The Bullets played against the San Diego Military All-Stars after the Padres-Dodgers game on June 22, 1994, at Jack Murphy Stadium and lost by a score of 4-0. Silver Bullets manager Phil Niekro explains to his catcher, Missy Cress, the fine art of catching a baseball. The highlight of Missy's career behind the dish was throwing out three runners in a game on August 21, 1995. One of the Bullets coaches was former Padres outfielder Johnny Grubb (1972–1976). (Larry Carpa.)

OH MY GWOSDZ. Padres catcher Doug Gwosdz attends a picnic for Junior Padres fans in the stands on May 22, 1982. His teammates nicknamed him "Eye Chart" because of the unusual spelling of his name. Doug's major-league career lasted four seasons (1981–1984), all with the Padres. His career totals include one homer and eight RBI, but on this day he was a big hit. (Madres.)

BROWN'S BRIDGE. This is the bridge from the Omni Hotel to PETCO Park. It should have a name, and my suggestion is that it should reflect the San Diego Padres' first player drafted for the 1969 team, Ollie Brown. It also signifies the most unique team color at the time: brown. (Fred O. Rodgers.)

MICHAEL MICKEY PETER DAVEY. For a period of time in the 1980s, the Padres would stage a concert a couple of times a season after a Sunday game. Many of those in attendance were not there to see the Padres play but rather the concert—the ball game was a bonus. The Padres had many concerts, hosting bands and singers such as the Beach Boys, the Doobie Brothers, the Charlie Daniels Band, Juice Newton, the Temptations, and the Four Tops. One of the fan favorites was when the Monkees came to town in 1986, the year they reunited. (Gary Holdinghausen.)

RESTLESS KIND. Tim Flannery is much more than a former major-leaguer or the current Giants third-base coach waving runners to home plate. He's a musician, and he has never forgotten his roots. Those roots include the Madres, who look forward to Tim playing for them whenever he can. (Madres.)

INSIDE BASEBALL. Ted Williams loved to talk about hitting with anyone. He especially got a kick sitting down with Tony Gwynn for the first time and firing questions about hitting to him. Gwynn admitted that he was slightly intimidated, as Ted had a booming voice and would ask challenging questions. Tony showed nothing but respect for Ted and always referred to him as Mr. Williams. Here, in 1992, Ted explains to Tony Gwynn that on an inside pitch, he should hit it out of the park. (Author's collection.)

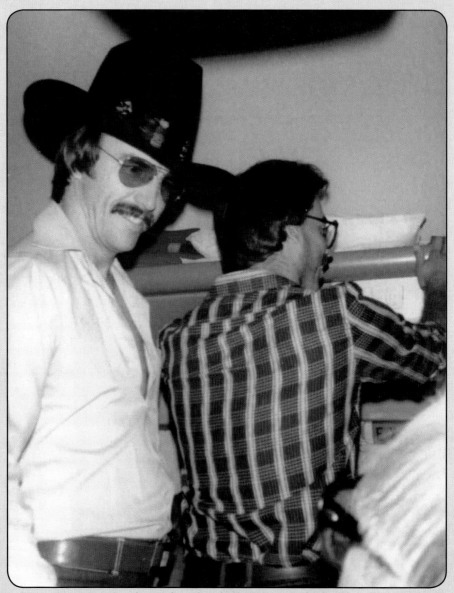

"DIRTY." Kurt Bevacqua was always about baseball. He was the batboy for Yankees during spring training in the 1960s having grown up in Florida. He picked up the nickname "Dirty Kurt" in the minors in reference to his uniform, and he won the 1975 major-league players bubble gum–blowing contest while with the Brewers. Kurt played for the Padres twice (1979–1980, 1982–1985). Each season he played for the Padres, his off-the-field experiences were not only astonishing but also entertaining. On a dare in 1982, Bevacqua caught five baseballs thrown from the Imperial Bank Building roof (325 feet above the street) in downtown San Diego and missed the sixth ball thrown from Terry Kennedy because he tried to catch it behind his back. He was one of 13 players thrown out of the August 12, 1984, game against the Braves in Atlanta as a result of going into the stands after a fan threw a cup of beer on him. Later that year, he hit a memorable homer in the World Series. He also had a verbal feud with Dodgers manager Tommy Lasorda that became an instant "radio-bleeped" recording and came out of the stands after his retirement during a Padres old-timers game to pinch hit. (Val Schiller.)

STRETCH MAKES IT. Willie McCovey is congratulated on his induction to the Baseball Hall of Fame in 1986 by Commissioner Peter Ueberroth when the ceremony was conducted on the side of the museum in Cooperstown, New York. McCovey, who was known as "Big Mac," started playing for the Padres in 1974, when Ray Kroc, who owned McDonald's, purchased the team. There is absolutely no link between McDonald's Big Mac and the Padres first baseman; McDonald's started selling and labeling its Big Macs in the late 1960s. McCovey was traded to Oakland during the 1976 season. (Bill Klink.)

A GIANT DODGER. Dave Winfield turned in front of a giant photograph of Dodgers great Jackie Robinson to look at me as he went down the steps toward the dugout-level seats at Dodger Stadium in 2010. Winfield never got to meet Jackie, but he has long been a student of the Negro Leagues and appreciative of what those before him did to blaze the trail. Dave once said that the greatest compliment he ever received was when "Cool Papa" Bell told him, "You could have played with us." (Randy Grossman.)

105

IN THE BLEACHERS. When the Winfield Pavilion program started, I was the Padres' coordinator and met with Dave's wonderful and very helpful friend and volunteer coordinator Dorothy Bowen, who was a delight to work with and very helpful. In the background, appropriately, was Dave's agent, Al Frohman. (Author's collection.)

PADRES DNA. This photograph of Dave Winfield and Sparky Anderson was taken during the Baseball Hall of Fame weekend in 2010, slightly more than three months before Sparky passed. It was the first time Winfield and Anderson saw each other that weekend, a greeting on the front steps of the Otesaga Hotel, where the Hall of Famers stayed during the weekend. Sparky (coach) and Dave (player and front-office executive) have the Padres as part of their baseball DNA. (Randy Grossman.)

BLIMP SHOT. I had a chance to get a ride in a Goodyear blimp in the early 1980s. When we floated over San Diego Stadium, I took out my camera and shot this picture. (J.C. Crouch.)

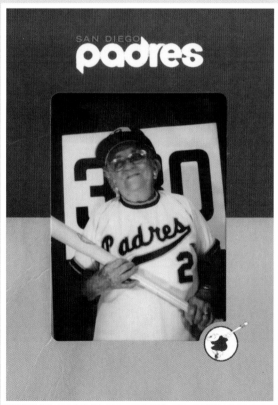

GRANDMA PADRE. The Padres had a setup at San Diego Stadium in 1977 where anyone could put on a Padres uniform and have a Polaroid photograph taken so that it looked like they were standing in front of the outfield fence. The photograph was then slipped into a paper frame that resembled a baseball card. My mother, Eleanor Hampson Depin, was a big Padres fan even though she was born in England and came to the United States when she was 13 years old. Here she is with the biggest grin on her face. Her favorite player was Padres outfielder Johnny Grubb. (John Hampson.)

GROWTH CHART. Growing up loving baseball has provided fans with benchmarks along the way. And, if they are photographic, they can be dramatic. Jacob Pomrenke, at age six (left, in 1988) and age 25 (right, in 2007), poses with Ted Williams's Hall of Fame plaque at the National Baseball Hall of Fame in Cooperstown, New York. (At left, Norman "Jake" Pomrenke; at right, Tracy Greer.)

SIXTY-ONE IS STILL THE RECORD. My six-year-old godson and the grandson of Roger Maris is about to go to the mound at Qualcomm Stadium and throw out the ceremonial first pitch prior to a Padres game in 1999. The occasion was to celebrate the US Postal Service issuing a stamp to commemorate Roger hitting 61 home runs in 1961. Andrew is wearing his grandfather's actual game-used New York Yankees 1961 jersey. (Author's collection.)

Ten

BORED—AND A SOUR NOTE

Hollywood mogul Tom Werner had owned the Padres for a very short time in 1990 when he called me to talk about enhancing the scheduled promotion of Working Women's Day. The underlying thought was to recognize and acknowledge the many and varied contributions of women in the home and in the workplace.

"Andy," said Tom, "what would you think if I could get Roseanne Barr to sing the national anthem for the game?" I thought the idea was great and said so and then had the temerity to ask Tom if she could sing. He replied quickly, "Of course, she's a professional." I countered by suggesting that she sing "Take Me Out To The Ball Game" in the seventh inning. It was not to be . . . Roseanne would sing "The Star Spangled Banner." I suggested we pre-record it and allow her to lip sync the song to avoid the brief third-of-a-second delay that San Diego Stadium's sound system encountered. Tom would have none of it: "She wants to sing it live, Andy."

Days before the game, Roseanne appeared as a guest on *The Tonight Show with Johnny Carson*, and the subject came up of her singing the national anthem for the upcoming Padres game. When asked to give the studio audience and national viewers a sample of her singing, Roseanne chose to belt out a few lines from "Kung Fu Fighting." Until the time she actually began to sing for Johnny, I assumed it would be a situation comparable to Jim Nabors, whose voice belied his looks and persona; I was wrong again. The next day, I explained to club president Dick Freeman what I had heard. I asked him to please have Tom Werner get us out of having Roseanne sing. According to Dick, Werner said not to worry about it. Yeah sure, don't worry about it. My career hung in the balance of Roseanne Barr's performance, and it was here before I knew it. The Padres public-address announcer, Bruce Binkowski, was introducing the Hollywood star and television personality Roseanne Barr: "Please rise and join Roseanne Barr in singing our National Anthem."

Fingernails scratching on a blackboard would be a Brahms's lullaby compared to the dissonant sounds of Roseanne Barr. She was so off-key, the melody was unrecognizable. Boos began to fill the stadium. The strong military presence at so many Padres games took the rendition by Barr as an insult and disrespectful.

To compound the disaster, Roseanne stuck her fingers in her ears not to silence the booing, but to avoid hearing the delay of her own voice over the PA system. Within seconds, the loosely described singing became screeching comparable to a barn full of young owlets. As she concluded—prompted by the suggestion of Padres catcher Mark Parent to do what all ballplayers do at the end of the anthem—Roseanne grabbed at her crotch and spit. The fans were livid, immediately believing Roseanne's gestures were mocking the Padres fans or the national anthem of the United States—or both. Simply put, that part of Working Women's Day was a bust.

LOVE AT FIRST SIGHT. I loved Lane Field, and I loved the scoreboard in center. I realize that after all these years, there was nothing special about it other than being the first professional baseball scoreboard I ever saw in person and that I spent a lot of time and the most enjoyable part of my childhood at the ballpark watching the greatest Padres players do remarkable things on the field. I snuck into the park and took this photograph one summer in the late 1940s. (Stacy Parker.)

IT'S TIME. Nothing was more exhilarating then when it was time for Trevor Hoffman to come in to pitch and protect a win for the Padres. The scoreboard lit up, and the public-address system rocked with AC/DC's "Hells Bells." The concept of playing the song when Hoffman entered a game was at the suggestion of Padres employee Chip Bowers, who had just started working for the team in the front office. (Madres.)

OH THOSE WALKS! The Padres were 20 games out of first place when the Astros came to town. It was the second game of a Sunday doubleheader against Houston with the score tied 5-5 on Sunday, June 30, 1974. The Padres had the bases loaded when Horace Clarke came to bat in the bottom of the 11th inning. The Astros' Jerry Johnson was facing Clarke, who was hitting .179, and walked him, "driving in" Nate Colbert from third base, and the Padres won 6-5. The scoreboard proclaims the victory! (Jack McDonald.)

A ROSE IS A ROSE. Pete Rose was a baseball superstar who hit a lot of singles. The San Diego Stadium scoreboard flashed in colored lights his image and his 3,000-hit milestone, which took place in Cincinnati against the Expos. Rose would break Ty Cobb's career hit record against the Padres seven years later, on September 11, 1985, also in Cincinnati. (Tom Larwin.)

CUB BUSTERS. The movie *Ghostbusters* was a hit in 1984, and so were the Padres. Radio station KFMB carried Padres games that season and rewrote the words to the *Ghostbusters* movie theme music and titled it "Cub Busters." It worked to customize their version to fit the occasion. The Padres won 6-3 on October 7 and represented the National League in the World Series. (Tom Larwin.)

OH SAY YOU CAN'T SING. On July 25, 1990, at 7:44 p.m., Roseanne Barr attempted to sing the National Anthem in between games of a Padres doubleheader. The winner of either game has long been forgotten (the Padres won both games against the Reds), but the nation remembers this musical catastrophe. This is what the scoreboard looked like at that very moment. (Jan Brooks.)

GO GREENE. The Padres new shortstop was Khalil Greene, and on September 6, 2003, he got his first hit in the first inning against the Astros, a single off Ron Villone. Greene was supposed to be the answer to all of the Padres' infield problems. He was going to play short for a long time, and that single was just the beginning of what everyone thought or hoped would be a career total of 2,700 to 3,000 hits. After seven years and 628 hits, Greene was gone due to the pressure and stress he felt playing baseball. (Madres.)

HAPPY BIRTHDAY, HOMER. Fans could order a birthday wish for a nominal fee, and it would be shown on the scoreboard during the Padres' game. Here birthday wishes are sent out to Homer, who was 11 on May 9, 1978. (Lucy Dickson.)

BORED. It appears that the Padres were not able to field a complete team on this August night in 1974, when the Braves were in town to play the Padres at San Diego Stadium. Only three positions are listed on the scoreboard: short, second, and a new position indicated by 2F. (Madres.)

NOW PITCHING. The 1978 All-Star Game at San Diego Stadium was in the bottom of the seventh inning when Ron Guidry of the New York Yankees came in to pitch and replace Jim Kern of the Cleveland Indians. With runners on first and second, "Louisiana Lightning" faced Willie Stargell of the Pittsburgh Pirates. After a passed ball and the runners moved up a base, "Pops" hit a fly ball to center to end the inning. (Peter Nunez.)

Eleven

SAFE AT HOME

San Diego has an incredible amount to offer baseball fans who are students of the game, devout historians, or casual observers.

It is almost impossible to travel around San Diego County and not see a subtle or dramatic reference to baseball. Not far from PETCO Park and down the right-field foul line a couple of blocks is the Baseball Research Center (BRC), located on the eighth floor of the San Diego Library. It houses a plethora of baseball research material that can only be comparable to the Baseball Hall of Fame Library in Cooperstown, New York. In 2014, the library, with the help of the local San Diego Ted Williams Chapter of the Society for American Baseball Research, acquired the rich and thorough research material of statistician and baseball historian Bill Weiss. Also featured on the walls of the BRC is a baseball Fantography exhibit.

Throughout the city, fans can find baseball landmarks, such as the original Pacific Coast League site of Lane Field, Albert Spalding's home, the field that Ted Williams played on as a kid, a college ballpark named after a former student and Padres icon Tony Gwynn, a statue to Padres broadcaster Jerry Coleman, and the plane he flew in combat at the Air and Space Museum in Balboa Park. Plus, on any given day, a current or retired professional baseball player can be found on one of the many first-class golf courses throughout San Diego County, having a meal at any of the fine restaurants, or skateboarding on a downtown street. The major-league Padres' original home, San Diego Stadium (now known as Qualcomm Stadium), is one of the few former major-league ballpark structures still standing and in use around the country and is used for NFL games. You may also want to check out the baseball exhibit at the Hall of Champions, located in Balboa Park. There are streets (Tony Gwynn Drive) and parkways (Ted Williams Parkway) in San Diego that acknowledge Padres greats, and many former players and baseball executives still make the city their home.

San Diego has produced dozens of professional baseball players who have left their marks on the sport and their community, dating back to Gavvy Cravath, a right fielder who played primarily for the Philadelphia Phillies and was born in Escondido in 1881, and extending to more recent players such as Alan Trammel, who grew up in San Diego and attended Kearny High School, and Cole Hamels, the left-handed pitcher for the Phillies who was born in San Diego and graduated from Rancho Bernardo High School.

"Baseball rich" is not a term that should or could be measured in dollars, nor is it to be measured in the number of World Series rings the "San Diego local nine" wins, but rather in the enjoyment generations of baseball fans receive from watching, reading, listening, playing, and remembering baseball.

San Diego County has been represented at the Little League World Series by these teams:

1952—San Diego National
1955—San Diego North Shore
1957—La Mesa Northern
1961—El Cajon/La Mesa Northern*
1977—El Cajon Western
1981—Escondido National
2001—Oceanside American
2005—Rancho Buena Vista
2009—Chula Vista Park View*
2013—Chula Vista Eastlake

*won the championship game

HAVE A BALL. Not far from the house that Ted Williams grew up in, there is a baseball field that he played on as a kid. It is appropriately named after him, and I could just imagine him grabbing his bat and glove as a kid and running to play ball from morning to night. (Spencer Kinyon.)

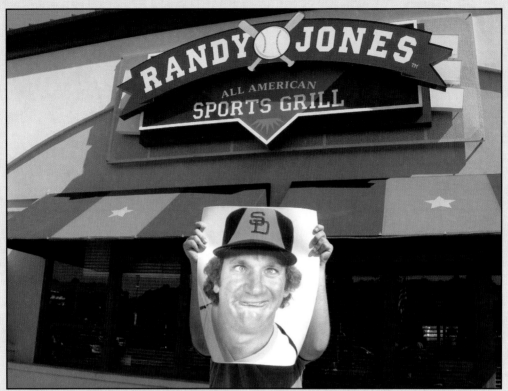

FACE TIME. Randy Jones owned and operated car washes in North County during the late 1970s. Jones is now in the restaurant and food business. He specializes in barbecue sauce and can be found when the Padres are out of town at his All-American Sports Grill, making sure that the Texas Leaguer burger, Cy Young burger, or Padre burger are cooked just right. I had my brother Sean hold this great picture of Randy making a funny face in front of the restaurant and went in to get it autographed. (Spencer Kinyon.)

TRACKING A HOMER. My cousin Dan Boyle, who is the president of the local San Diego Ted Williams Chapter of the Society for American Baseball Research, stands in front of a large mural of Lane Field (under construction in 1936) located on Tenth Avenue in San Diego. Dan is pointing to the railroad tracks where legend has it that home runs bounced onto trains and travelled up to Los Angeles. (Roger Kerr.)

PERFECT PITCH. Joe Rathburn is an accomplished guitar player and singer. Prior to all Padres home games, he can be found at the Tin Fish restaurant, located on the west side of PETCO Park, serenading fans who stop by for a bite to eat or throw down a couple of drinks. Joe sings an assortment of baseball songs, plus he somehow put music to "Casey at the Bat." I'm sure he takes requests. (Spencer Kinyon.)

THUMPER'S HOUSE. Ted Williams grew up in San Diego and lived at 4121 Utah Street. While he played for the Boston Red Sox, he lived in a hotel rather than in a house or apartment for many years during the baseball season. It is not unusual every now and then to see fans of the "Splendid Splinter" snap a picture of the house he grew up in. (Bill Klink.)

AZTECS FOREVER. Tony Gwynn and Doug Harvey both attended San Diego State growing up. They both played on the college team, and they are both members of the National Baseball Hall of Fame in Cooperstown. Doug was an ump and called balls and strikes, while Tony was a hitter who hit balls that were strikes. (Author's collection.)

MEMORY LANES. In 1961, Duke Snider Lanes bowling alley in Falbrook, California, opened. During the summer, the place was packed with people. I don't know how many of them were bowling enthusiasts, but the place had an air-conditioner that worked great. (Jack and Susie Nopal.)

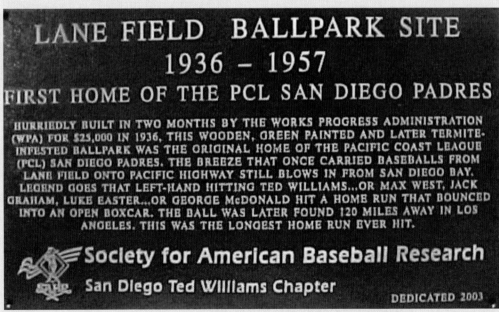

X MARKS THE SPOT. This plaque is located on the corner of Broadway and Pacific Coast Highway in downtown San Diego, where Lane Field used to stand. The field was the home of the Pacific Coast League Padres from 1936 to 1957. The last line of the marker recounts the longest homer ever hit. (Tom Larwin.)

NO ARMY FATIGUED. The Padres trainer from 1976 to 1990 was Dick Dent, who was known as "LT" because of the time he spent serving in the Army during the Vietnam War. Dent was renowned for his abilities to keep players healthy and on the field, get them in shape, and mentally prepare them for games. This is the plaque at the Mount Soledad Veterans Memorial in La Jolla, not far from Jerry Coleman's plaque for his service to our country. (Spencer Kinyon.)

GOOD DIRECTION. Ted Williams, who grew up in San Diego, was honored with a parkway in 1992. Ted said he used to hunt rabbits in that area many years ago as a kid. City official Ron Roberts is part of the ceremony. (Larry Carpa.)

A Real Sport. One of the most beautiful buildings overlooking the Pacific Ocean was once the home of Albert G. Spalding. Spalding was a pitcher, manager, and team executive who initiated a baseball world tour that traveled to Australia, Egypt, Italy, and Paris. He also started a sporting-goods business that is still operating and carries his name. While those accomplishments are impressive, Albert did them all before 1900. His home, which was built in 1901, still stands on the grounds of Point Loma Nazarene University. The building combines late-Victorian wooden architecture with historical motifs, such as the modified Corinthian column (now shaped like a papyrus leaf) and flattened arches. It was at this home where Spalding wrote the history of "Base Ball" in 1911. (Leslie Hanson.)

What a Relief. The 1963 Angels have been given credit for being the first team to introduce transporting bullpen relievers to the mound in a golf cart. Shortly after the idea caught on, teams designed the cart to look like a baseball with a cap on it. I'm guessing that sitting underneath the Padres cap in this 1972 image are relievers Freddie Norman and Gary Ross. Isn't it time the Padres bring back this intimidating and very retro means of bringing in the team's stoppers? (Larry McNaughton.)

CHARLIE HORSE. Gravesites are not always marked with a footstone or headstone. Consider the case of Joseph L. Quest, who was born on November 16, 1852, in New Castle, Pennsylvania, and died on November 14, 1924, in San Diego. Quest was a professional baseball player who would make an impact on all of sports that is still very much felt to this day. Joseph played for the White Stockings, Browns, Wolverines, Blues, and Athletics between 1871 and 1886. The son of a blacksmith, he had noticed that certain leg muscle injuries in baseball make the player who is injured walk like the old white horse, Charlie, that resided in his father's shop. Legend has it that in 1882, Quest was the first person to use the term "Charlie horse" for such an ailment. He is buried at Mount Hope Cemetery in San Diego. Unfortunately, poor Joe doesn't have a marker over his grave. With respect, I placed a used baseball over his grave and took a snapshot. Rest in peace, Joe. (Author's collection.)

IT WAS MILLER TIME. Bob Miller was a right-handed pitcher who played in the big leagues, beginning in 1957. His given name was Robert Lane Gemeinweiser but changed his last name to Miller. His career began with the St. Louis Cardinals in 1957 and finished in 1974 with the New York Mets. Along the way, Miller pitched for 10 teams, including his hometown Padres in 1971 and 1973. As crazy as it sounds, when he pitched for the Mets, there was another pitcher named Bob Miller on the team—but he was a left-hander. The left-handed Miller was 2-2 that year, pitching in 17 games, while the right-handed Miller was 1-12 in 33 games. The right-handed Miller also managed the Padres minor-league affiliate club, the Amarillo Gold Sox, in 1976, when the club finished in first place and won the league championship over the Shreveport Captains. His life was tragically cut short by an automobile accident in 1993, and he is buried in Dearborn Memorial Park in Poway, California. (Spencer Kinyon.)

ONE FOR THE BOOKS. The new San Diego Central Library that opened in the fall of 2013 has one of the most extensive collections of baseball research material in the country. The local San Diego Ted Williams Chapter of the Society for American Baseball Research established the Baseball Research Center on the eighth floor of the library. The collection maintains baseball material from the late 1800s up to the present. For the opening of the library, a display of baseball Fantography images was exhibited. (John Freeman.)

THE POWER ALLEY. A number of hidden baseball art pieces are scattered around the city. This one is located between two buildings on Tenth and Eleventh Avenues near PETCO Park. This is not a work of art that you would casually stroll by and notice; you have to look for it, and it's not that easy to find! (Lindsay Campbell.)

BASEBALL AT THE HALL. San Diego's Hall of Champions, located in Balboa Park, has a portion of the museum devoted to San Diego professional baseball. The exhibit features those who played for the PCL Padres and the major-league team. Also included are players who were born and/or grew up in San Diego County—everyone from Ray Boone to Pete Coscarart to Eric Karros. One of the highlights of the exhibit is the Tony Gwynn tribute, which includes the eight silver bats he won for having the best batting average in the National League. (Arnie Cardillo.)

IN PLANE SIGHT. Padres broadcaster Jerry Coleman accomplished much on the baseball field, in the dugout, and broadcast booth. He played and starred for the Yankees (he won Rookie of the Year in 1949 and World Series MVP in 1950), and he managed the Padres in 1980. His broadcasting career included the Yankees, CBS Radio, and the Padres, but the thing he was most proud of was the time he served as a Marine pilot in World War II and the Korean War. An exact replica of the F4U Corsair that Jerry flew in Korea is on display at the San Diego Air and Space Museum in Balboa Park. "LTCOL Jerry Coleman" is stenciled under the cockpit. Sitting next to the Corsair is a SBD Dauntless dive-bomber that he piloted in World War ll. Jerry flew 120 missions, earning him two Distinguished Flying Crosses, 13 Air Medals, and three Navy citations. He retired from the US Marine Corps with the rank of lieutenant colonel. (Both, Peter Briante.)

JERRY'S GOT OUR BACK. The Padres opener was March 30, 2014, and they beat the Dodgers 3-1. There was a moving pre-game tribute to the Padres' beloved broadcaster, Jerry Coleman, who passed away at the beginning of 2014 at the age of 89. As the largest crowd to ever attend a game at PETCO Park entered the ballpark, they were each given a special commemorative camouflage Padres T-shirt that had Jerry's initials on the back inside a star. The guy in front of me must have stood up a million times during the game and blocked my view of the field, but all I could do was smile because I was looking at a star for Jerry. (Al Treadwell.)

PRETTY PLEASE. The playing field at PETCO Park is well manicured and one of the best fields in major-league baseball. The groundskeepers take an enormous amount of pride in their work and very politely posted a sign requesting that the public when visiting the field should not step on the grass. (Madres.)

DISCOVER THOUSANDS OF LOCAL HISTORY BOOKS
FEATURING MILLIONS OF VINTAGE IMAGES

Arcadia Publishing, the leading local history publisher in the United States, is committed to making history accessible and meaningful through publishing books that celebrate and preserve the heritage of America's people and places.

Find more books like this at
www.arcadiapublishing.com

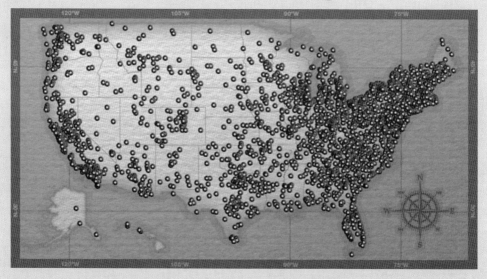

Search for your hometown history, your old stomping grounds, and even your favorite sports team.